The Design of Learning Spaces

Also available from Continuum

Regenerating Schools – Malcolm Groves

Schools and Communities – John West-Burnham, Maggie Farrar & George Otero

The Design of Learning Spaces

Pamela Woolner
Future Schools

Continuum International Publishing Group
The Tower Building
11 York Road
London
SE1 7NX

80 Maiden Lane Suite 704
New York NY 10038

www.continuumbooks.com

British Library Cataloguing-in-Publication Data
A catalogue record for this book is available from the British Library.

ISBN: 9781855397743 (paperback)

Library of Congress Cataloging-in-Publication Data

Typeset by Fakenham Photosetting Ltd, Fakenham, Norfolk
Printed and bound in Great Britain by Antony Rowe

Contents

Acknowledgements

I would like to thank all the students and staff at the various schools I have worked with and visited over the last few years for sharing their experiences and insights. I also acknowledge with thanks the contribution of the funders of the various research projects which take me into schools and colleges across the UK. In particular, though, I am extremely grateful to all my colleagues in the Research Centre for Learning and Teaching at Newcastle University for the fruitful collaborations which are so central to our approach.

Preface

After many years of minimal investment in school premises, we are in the midst of a wave of planning, building and using new schools. This includes all English secondary schools, being renewed through Building Schools for the Future (BSF), as well as schemes for English primaries and programmes of school construction in Scotland and Wales.

Initially this produced great excitement and the drawing of parallels with Victorian idealism and post-war optimism. Yet as time goes on there are also murmuring of disappointment and scepticism. Partly this is a problem of timing, but it also reflects genuine difficulties, challenges and misunderstandings. A central feature is the necessity, when designing a school, of people with backgrounds in design and architecture talking to people with backgrounds in education. Despite genuine attempts to speak the same language, this is difficult when underlying knowledge and unspoken assumptions are very different. To ease this tension on the architects' side, Mark Dudek, an architect and academic, in 2000 wrote a book, 'The Architecture of Schools', which he intended to explain something of the educational side of school design to architects. This seems necessary, given the inevitable involvement of architects in planning new schools, but not sufficient in light of the need felt by many in architecture, education and government for a school's users to be involved in its design.

There seems to be a clear need, therefore, to consider current issues in the design of learning environments, starting from an educational perspective, aiming at those who use schools and who would like to think more about how spaces in them might be planned and arranged to facilitate learning and teaching. This book is a contribution to such exploration.

1 Four schools through time

Introduction

Learning can take place anywhere. Educators are aware that learners are not empty vessels, but come to school with understandings derived from their wider lives. Unexpected informal learning can take place in all sorts of apparently unlikely situations. So does the detail of the physical surroundings provided by schools in fact matter?

This simplistic phrasing hides the sense that most people have, and which I think can be rationally justified, that the physical environment does make a difference. We need to be quite careful, however, in assessing how much difference and of what sort. Although a particular learning environment does not determine the teaching and learning that takes place there, it can clearly help or hinder specific activities or sorts of use. To consider this relationship between design and use in a less abstract way, this introductory chapter will look at four notable school buildings constructed during the latter half of the twentieth century. They were all designed to facilitate learning, but against differing background understandings of how this should be done. It is interesting to question how they have stood the test of time, through changing relationships between architecture and education, and whether it is possible to generalise from them any principles of school design, or, perhaps, less ambitiously, methods of school designing.

Background issues in school building

The planning and building of schools is affected by a range of factors; some general societal variables, such as demographic and economic influences, and some specific to architecture or to education. These factors, characterised as direct influences on eras of school construction or as more vague background issues, are illustrated in Figure 1.1.

These factors influence both the timing of particular bursts of school-building and the styles of the resulting schools. Thus, for example, in the UK, as elsewhere in Europe, rebuilding after World War Two (WW2), coupled with the 1950s' high birth rate, precipitated a wave of school-building, while new building methods, such as prefabrication,

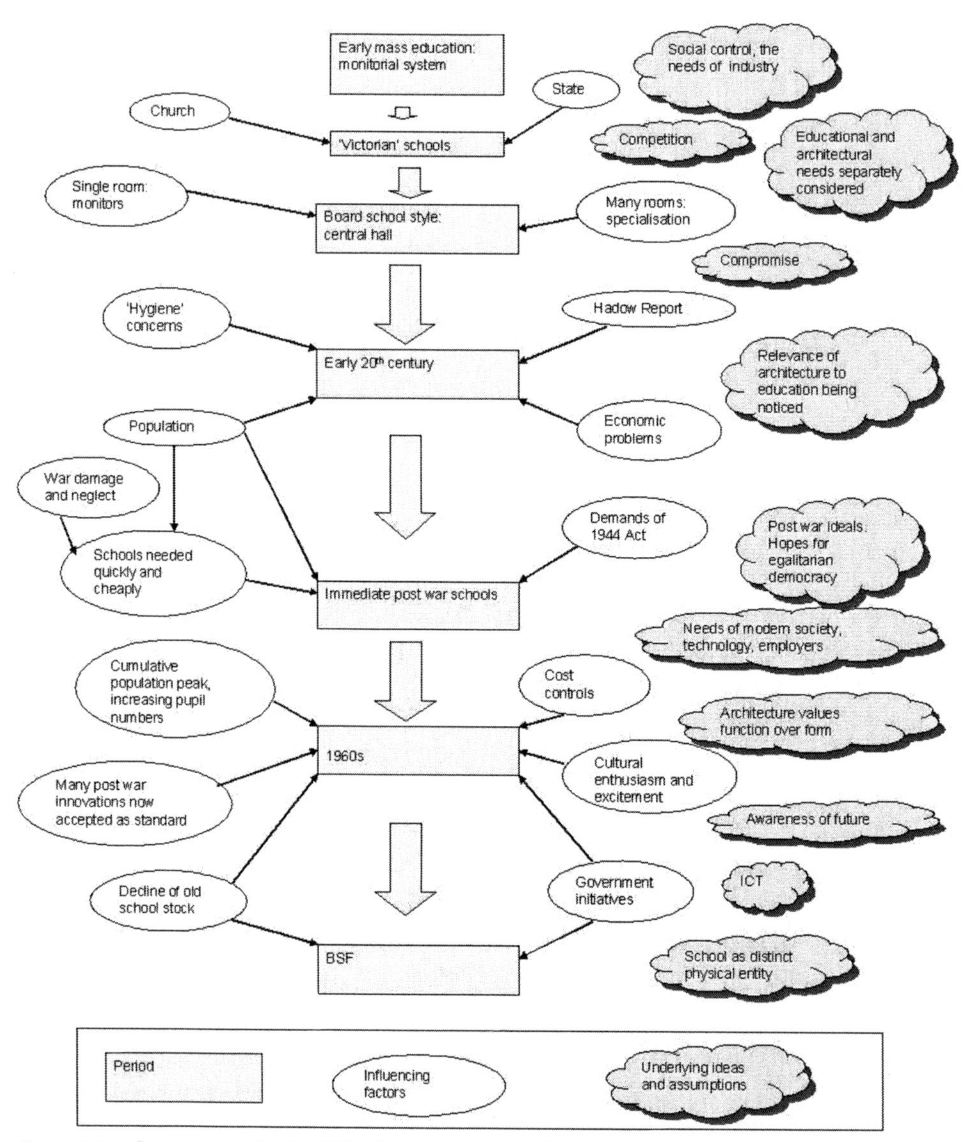

Figure 1.1 Influences on school building in the UK over the last two centuries

impacted on the design of schools. Through the 1950s and '60s a number of educational needs and desires also affected school style, from the requirement that the new post-war secondary 'modern' schools include workshops and space for other practical activities to a growing desire among educationalists of the 1960s that primary school buildings should be designed to facilitate a more child-centred approach to learning.

Sketched in this manner, the influences on a school building, although numerous, might seem fairly explicable and discrete. However, these factors will of course all interact, and, related to this interaction, is the fact that underlying all the individual influences are the general societal assumptions, ideals and related understandings which impact on conceptions of education and of architecture. Detailed consideration of school buildings of any period tends to reveal this underlying complexity (Woolner *et al.*, 2005), and this allows particular epochs to continue to be argued over and reassessed as time passes. For example, the precursors to the move to open plan designs for UK primary schools has generated a considerable literature from Pearson (1972), through Seaborne and Lowe (1977) and Cooper (1981), to Saint (1987).

Against this complex background, certain individual school buildings are considered particularly notable and might be referred to as iconic. Such labelling brings with it its own confusions and arguments, but, it might be hoped, can also reveal deeper understanding of the process through which all school buildings are designed, used and ultimately evaluated. Although such notable schools might exemplify the complexity of requirements and reactions as time passes, examining them might also help to illuminate general aspects of the learning environment and so add to knowledge of good practice in school design.

Some iconic UK schools

Four notable UK schools, built at different times, but still in use, will now be individually described and discussed. They have all been referred to as notable from their construction, when those involved were often consciously aware of the schools' distinctive status, and then through changing times. These are the schools that are reliably mentioned by historic accounts of British school building, whether from an educational or an architectural perspective (for an example of the former, see Maclure, 1985; for the latter, see Saint, 1987). As will be shown, their users tend to remain somewhat aware, even as the years pass, of their school's distinctiveness and this colours their appreciation of the buildings.

The schools considered below are spread through recent history, from an example of immediate post-war renewal, Burleigh School, to an instance of more recent school design, Woodlea School. As will become clear, these buildings are notable for differing complexes of reasons, with some centring more on architectural and built features of their design while others derive more from educational and organisation aspects.

The schools were chosen because of repeated references to them in both contemporaneous and historical accounts of school buildings from the immediate post-war period through to recent work. It is possible to get a sense of current usage and viewpoints by reading the school and related websites and by visiting the schools. Comments made by the headteacher on a brief questionnaire sent out in 2006 provide a snapshot of school concerns and views some years after the building was designed, as well as indicating trajectories of change and development.

Burleigh Primary School, Cheshunt, Herfordshire

Origins

Burleigh School in Herfordshire (Herts), built 1946–48, was one of the very first of the post-war wave of schools and it was designed and built against a background of severe shortages of labour and materials.

While other Local Education Authorities (LEAs) were struggling to plan and design appropriate schools, Herts employed a group of innovative and enthusiastic young architects, who designed a system of parts, many pre-fabricated off-site, which could be put together with minimum labour to produce a range of school layouts. Although this was partly a rational reaction to post-war shortages, this building style also fitted with the ambitions of many to break with the past and forge a new post-war world (for a flavour of this desire, see the account of Saint, 1987). As Herts school architect, Bruce Martin, opined, it was thought desirable to build 'lightly for a life of free and changing activity' (1952: 18). Such sentiments included, however, an economic side, which might be seen as negative, and which is revealed by Martin's further comment that, 'Every section of the building needs to be overhauled with a view to reducing costs' (1952: 18).

With rather more hindsight, Saint (1987) argues that such apparent meanness was justified by the need to share limited resources with, for instance, the construction of housing (p.66–67) and was ameliorated by the determination of the school designers to divert money from architectural features and the 'look of the building' to spend on lighting, colour landscaping aand works of art (p.234).

Therefore, when Burleigh infant School was completed in 1947 it was notable for being an initial system-built school, but also for the ideas and convictions it embodied, and for the 'modern' style which would come to define the post-war school as well as other public buildings (Bullock, 2002). However, it is worth noting that although in some ways Burleigh represented a break with the past, in many respects it was quite traditional and even some of its modern features show a continuity with the past. The extensive glazing and outdoor access from the classrooms refer back to the design of the few schools built during the 1930s, and this preoccupation with light and outdoor space can be seen as originating in the early twentieth century drive for light and ventilation (see Seaborne and Lowe, 1977, for discussion; Robson, 1911 for contemporaneous examples of such architecture).

Furthermore, the organisation of Burleigh is based on traditional self-contained classrooms, arranged along corridors. Such corridors had become the norm in the school design of the proceeding two decades, but they were curtailed soon afterwards by spending limits which encouraged more clustered designs. Within the classroom, efforts were made to provide a more child-friendly environment than formerly, with low windows and child-sized furnishings. Yet the school was organised on the basis of separate rooms, each containing a class of similar aged children and a single teacher, in the manner which had become accepted towards the end of the nineteenth century (Seaborne & Lowe, 1977).

Change and development

Although, as will be discussed further below, some alterations have been made to Burleigh Primary School over its lifetime, the school building is essentially quite unchanged, as can be seen from the school website (Burleigh, 2009). The layout is unaltered and the school still sits within plenty of open space, while, in the classrooms, evidence of the innovative steel frame construction method can be seen. Even the recent improvements noted on the website of 'apparatus for the junior playground' and 'redecoration of all junior classrooms' can be seen as building on the original priority given to outdoor space and continuing to emphasise the sparing yet vibrant decorative style.

An important aspect of the construction which has not fared so well, though, is the exterior, concrete cladding. As Saint (1987; p.95) describes, the early system-built schools experienced many problems with cladding and the cladding at Burleigh has been replaced (for details, see Kingsbury, 2006). The engineer who carried out this work notes that 'most of the rest of the building is in good condition' and points out that he was able to replace the cladding with panels of the same external dimensions, so preserving the original design, but which are thicker to give improved strength and insulation.

Figure 1.2 Recent aerial view of Burleigh (from school website http://www.burleigh.herts.sch.uk/)

Figure 1.3 Newly clad buildings at Burleigh (Kingsbury, 2006)

This sounds undeniably positive, but the disadvantages of such attention to detail, necessitated by the school's architectural status, is conveyed by the head teacher's comment in 2006 that 'Grade II listed status causes problems: like for like replacements very expensive and time consuming (paperwork, etc.)'.

Other remarks made by the head teacher at this time are also revealing. In answer to the question, 'In what, if any, way was your school building considered notable when it was first opened?' he replies that it was the 'first (or one of the first) 'system-build' schools after 2nd World War. Noted for its spaciousness, architecturally-striking design and green field space'. This shows awareness within the school even now of its history and significance. The head further comments that a difficulty with the building is that 'as there is a lot of glass it gets hot' and mentions, among alterations made, that 'some cloakrooms [have been] knocked out to provide class space'.

Therefore the problems with the building, and alterations which have been made, seem to be typical of the shortcomings which have come to light over time with such designs and the changes that have occurred in school design, sometimes in response to such deficiencies and sometimes reflecting changing priorities in education. Thus recently built schools are unlikely to give over so much space to non-teaching purposes, such as corridors and cloakrooms, and glazing tends to be less extensive with designs showing more awareness of over-heating.

These problems acknowledged, however, Burleigh's head in 2006 concluded then that the building 'still stands up as a functional building nearly 60 years on', a view which would seem to concur with the upbeat message suggested by the school website.

Finmere Primary School, Oxfordshire

Origins

Finmere Primary School was built in 1959, but, in contrast to Burleigh, its design was led less by architectural factors and aims than by educational ideals and the perceived demand of the developing primary curriculum. It was a small village school and its external design is simple and understated (see Figure 1.4), but its internal organisation made it extremely distinctive and perhaps revolutionary. The two classrooms and shared hall space could be combined or separated in differing ways, using folding partitions, while, within the classroom, space was divided into bays for various activities. This design supported the more fluid, child-centred approach to teaching and learning then being favoured by progressive educationalists.

Although the collaboration of educators (from the LEA) and architects (from the Ministry of Education) to produce a space to facilitate such practice was emphasised at the time, it has been pointed out since (by e.g. Maclure, 1985 and Saint, 1987) that the practical requirements of teaching a small population of 5 to 11 year olds necessitates regroupings, variously sized groups and children of different ages working together. Therefore the design can be seen as both exemplifying general contemporaneous ideals about school organisation and providing a practical solution to the needs of Finmere's children. Evaluations since the school was built have tended to emphasise one or other of these aspects, but it can be seen that both are important.

Change and development

The local history website (Finmere, nd) devotes considerable space to Finmere School and manages to convey both the educational ideals and the practical needs served by the school design. The introductory section to the school claims that, in Oxfordshire, teachers' 'enthusiasm inspired the architects to design a school that met teachers' and pupils' needs. This included rethinking the conventional classroom'. Reference is then made to the particular problems of rural schools and the fact that 'space was needed for small groups of pupils, as well as for the collective work of classes of twenty-five pupils'.

Also of note, from this website, is the implication that Finmere is still understood locally as a distinctive school, which the local historian describes as 'groundbreaking'.

Figure 1.4 View of Finmere School (Andy Boddington) from the local history website

Such an impression is supported by a recent head teacher's reply to the question of how the school was regarded when first built:

> I believe that Finmere School was very well accepted by its own users when it opened in 1960. In addition educators from all over Europe came to visit the school and were impressed by its design.

The head teacher's comments, however, also reveal some interesting contemporary reactions to the design, including changes which have been made or are desired. She likes the interlinked organisation of the classrooms and points out that 'no corridors means there is no wasted space or behaviour problems when moving from one area of the school to another'. Yet, she says, 'We no longer open up the concertina doors and work in an 'open-plan' way. Teachers found the noise level too high when working in this way and also behaviour issues increased'. Furthermore, it is notable that the recent return to more whole class teaching in UK primary schools has made the subdivisions within the classrooms awkward, causing problems such as 'where to put the interactive white boards' and provoking the on-going removal of some of the dividing walls within the classrooms.

Underlining the fact that the distinctiveness of Finmere continues to be related to organisational, rather than architectural, features, the headteacher only refers twice to more purely physical aspects of the building. She comments that 'the original copper roof leaked badly and was replaced two years ago' and notes the serendipitous fact that 'all light switches at child height which is fantastic for the requirement now for schools to make the environment fully accessible for wheel chair users'.

Eveline Lowe Primary School, Southwark, London

Origins

Opened in 1966, Eveline Lowe represented the conscious development of school space appropriate to the educational ideals and pedagogical practice associated with Finmere. These ideas about primary education were increasingly being expressed and would underlie many of the conclusions of the Plowden report of 1967 (England, 1967), which was later seen as the 'highpoint of progressive influence' (Jones, 2003: 84). The design of Eveline Lowe took many of the elements of the Finmere plan and extended them to produce an open plan school intended for a much bigger, urban, school population. Aspects of Finmere, such as the bays designed for different activities feature in the layout of Eveline Lowe, together with features, already noted, which had become common in all post-war schools, such as outdoor access from classrooms and plenty of low-down windows. The school opened with considerable fanfare and media coverage, and the design was understood as being a key part of Eveline Lowe's intention of being at the forefront of progressive primary education. Many of the photographs taken during its first years of operation are intended to show the open-plan design being used to facilitate child-centred pedagogy.

It was clearly intended that the school should act as a prototype to be emulated across the UK. In some senses, this did indeed happen as the primary school-building burst of the 1960s and early 1970s (which actually saw more schools built than the immediate post-war wave: see Woolner *et al.*, 2005: 16) resulted in schools that tended to be somewhat open-plan. By 1976, an architecture reference book (Mills, 1976) was able to assume open planning as the norm for primary schools and all the recently built schools provided as examples in the book were designed in this way.

Yet paralleling the increasing prevalence of open-plan schools was the development of complaints about using them. A report by the National Union of Teachers (NUT England, 1974) and the detailed survey of Bennett *et al.* (1980) note some of the problems. These include noise levels, teachers lacking specific training for this environment and worries that for some children open-plan spaces might be inappropriate, producing behaviour problems and lack of involvement. There is now a considerable body of research, from the UK and US, which examines how open-plan schools are actually used and a major conclusion is that the design does not determine the teacher's practice, with wide variations in how open-plan space is used (Gump, 1975; Rivlin and Rothenberg, 1976; McMillan, 1983).

However, while a building might not dictate teaching practice, it can help or hinder it, and this will be particularly problematic if, as surveys carried out in the 1970s and '80s began to suggest, the majority of teachers continue to teach in a traditional way. It is this mismatch of the pedagogical intentions of the architecture and the practice of the teachers that some commentators at the time were most critical of (see Cooper, 1981). It can be argued that, by systematically exaggerating the move towards 'progressive' educational practices, the educationalists who advised the architects misled them into believing that a particular style of teaching had become the norm and required appropriate buildings. More moderately, there are inevitable difficulties in trying to distinguish a genuine development in education from the activity of an adventurous few that will never catch on. At the time, this was not helped by the tendency of architects to meet teachers and LEA advisors at the vanguard of educational practice. A contemporaneous example of this is provided by educationalist Eric Pearson's recommendation that architects engage with 'those teachers at the spearhead of educational innovation' (Pearson, 1975: 46).

Change and development

Despite the problems that came to be associated with schools of this type, however, and the general reaction against the progressive, individualised teaching style which they were intended to support, Eveline Lowe remained a successful and welcoming school. A visit by the author to the school in 2005 was revealing. The building appeared to have matured successfully and the courtyard gardens, which were rather open and bleak-looking in the early pictures, were full of a variety of plants and trees. A visiting teacher from another part of the UK commented in surprise at the continued satisfaction with the general layout of the school, saying that such open-plan schools in her area were generally considered to be failures.

The explanation for this could lie in the fact that Eveline Lowe School was something of an original, with later copies becoming increasingly formulaic, ill-considered and lazily implemented. This is suggested by the examination by Bennett *et al.* (1980: 222–230) of the design of a school built in 1975, which reveals the inevitability of circulation problems and suggests a slap-dash approach to the school's architecture with a by then fairly standard open-plan design rolled out without much thought. Furthermore, a careful examination of plans of schools built during the 1960s and '70s (included e.g. in Maclure, 1985 and Saint, 1987) reveals that Eveline Lowe encompasses a greater area than many other schools built during this time. Since both the reports of Bennett *et al.* (1980) and the NUT (1974) emphasise the importance of enough space in primary schools, this could be a vital factor in Eveline Lowe's continued success.

Woodlea Primary School, Borden, Hampshire

Origins

After the prolonged high rates of the 1950s and '60s, birth rates in the UK declined in the 1970s, staying low through the 1980s and '90s. This was among the reasons why, in most areas, very few new schools have been built over the last two to three decades. However, due to population movement, Hampshire was one of the few regions where decline in school age children has been less pronounced and this Local Authority (LA) has been notable for building a number of schools over the past twenty years.

As an interview with Hampshire's chief architect reveals (Curtis, 2003), the LA architects pride themselves on consulting the local community and building each school as an individual solution to a particular situation. Considering their work shows that they have been successful in creating both primary and secondary schools, each of which is quite distinctive and far from being versions of the same scheme.

Perhaps best known of these schools, is Woodlea Primary School, opened in1991. The challenge here was to build a school on a sloping, wooded site, while retaining the original landscape and sense of place. Architect Mark Dudek was extremely impressed with the building, commenting that it 'is a predominantly timber and masonry structure put together simply, with a stock of straightforward details which nevertheless encapsulate essential site-specific characteristics [...] No plan or photograph can do full justice to the poetic quality of this building in its natural setting' (Dudek, 2000: 152–153).

Change and development

When Woodlea was first built, it was considered to be quite singular and striking, and indeed it won design awards, but as time has progressed some of its features have come to seem more standard. Perhaps one reason for this is that the low number of schools built during the 1990s in the UK would tend to make any example from this period seem more distinct. It seems fair to conclude, however, that Woodlea was ahead of then current trends in some ways and included some features which have since become more common, perhaps partly as a result of their inclusion in Woodlea School.

In particular, care was taken with lighting and ventilation, making use of pitched glazing and natural ventilation to ensure good levels of light without overheating in the summer. Such systems of passive ventilation are increasingly seen as desirable, given recent, growing concerns about environmental impact, and feature in modern school designs (see e.g. DfES, 2004).

The head teacher's recent response to questions about the school building shows that the setting and general design of the school are still valued highly. She comments that 'Grounds / setting are unique! Much woodland' and notes that of interest about the building is that it is 'Impressive and different to look at' and 'The way it fits into the environment'.

However, despite Dudek's conviction that 'care has been taken to achieve a good acoustic environment in what is generally an open plan building' (2000: 152–153), Woodlea's head in 2006 cites 'acoustics' as one problem with the building, along with 'tiled floors in classes', which may well be related. This perhaps reflects a perennial difficulty with a more open-plan design, but also probably relates to the current preference for more whole class teaching, which was noted in considering Finmere, where contemporary concerns centre on difficulties with open-plan arrangements.

Since Woodlea was built, it has also been considered necessary to extend the reception classroom (which caters for 4 to 5 year olds in their first year of formal education) and provide additional storage space for the caretaker. There are various suggestions in the comments of the head teacher that interior space is limited, although she notes positively that the 'decking around building [provides] extra outside space'. It could be argued that area has been minimised, with the typical classrooms quite small at $42m^2$, but there is additional shared space between classrooms as well as the outside space. Furthermore, the head's remark that the reception classroom was extended after 'Two Ofsted reports cited the facilities / space as inadequate to deliver the curriculum' suggests that expectations of reception class activity might have increased since the school was built. Certainly over this time there has been an increased emphasis, coming from central government, on literacy and numeracy teaching in primary schools.

School design issues and iconic buildings

This chapter began by recognising that any school premises reflect the assumptions and aspirations of their times. In addition, however, it was anticipated that considering some schools built over a range of eras might shed light on more general aspects of the school environment, providing ideas for those currently involved with school design. There is considerable disagreement and conflicting ideas about what makes a successful school environment (Higgins *et al.*, 2005; Woolner *et al.*, 2007a), which will be considered further in Chapters 2 and 3. This confusion is exacerbated by both a lack of appropriate research into the physical learning environment (Clark, 2002) and, it can be argued, a failure to understand the lessons of history (Woolner *et al.*, 2005; CABE, 2006). Therefore any ideas generated by this brief consideration of a sample of exemplar schools should be beneficial.

Three principles for understanding how schools are judged over time

What do the evolving views of these older schools tell us about how a school built or refurbished now is likely to be judged by its users as time goes by? Are there general ways of proceeding with the design process, or aspects that should be included in the physical structure, if the school is to be considered to be a success?

Value of community recognition

Considering the iconic schools, any community participation or shared understanding of objectives would seem to bode well for a newly built school. It has been noted that all the iconic schools described above were recognised as special when they were opened and the continued awareness of their users of this status suggests that they enjoy some recognition and appreciation within their communities. In certain cases, there is clear evidence of long-term pride in the achievements of the school's architects, often tied to the locality. So the Finmere history society website comments that 'Oxfordshire was an ideal location to develop a groundbreaking school' (Finmere, 2006), while a recent head at Burleigh mentions being the 'first' system-built school. Although such figurehead status can have its disadvantages, it would seem generally beneficial. Therefore, any way that a school design process can draw in the community and encourage them to see the resulting building as a special and singular solution to their needs is likely to contribute to a continued favourable response to the school.

Importance of good design

This is not to suggest, however, that the continued valuing of a school is determined by the clever management of people and information. There is evidence from the iconic schools that they each embody clear, quite ambitious, overall design values as well as thoughtful individual features. For example, at Eveline Lowe teaching area is adequate, while Woodlea is designed to complement its immediate environment. There is evidence of attention to detail in all the schools considered with, for instance, the care taken to achieve a child-centred environment at Finmere having the unforeseen benefit of putting light switches at an appropriate level for wheelchair users.

It is notable, however, that the iconic schools discussed, though all primary schools, differ in appearance and are quite different in their layouts and organisation, suggesting that there is no complete solution to school design. This suggests their designs cannot be used to prescribe features for new schools, but there might be some generalisations to be made, alongside the suggestion made above of the importance of high design values and careful construction. It could be argued that all the iconic school buildings involve a sense of linkage between the interior classroom and the outside environment. They all have many windows, including low down, small-child-height windows, and the designs centre on the use of natural light. All the designs include easy outside access, often to patio or veranda areas, with these areas being central features of the design at Woodlea, Burleigh and Eveline Lowe.

Evaluation continues over time

A clear conclusion from the investigation of iconic schools is that the nature of the evaluation of a school building is not that of an individual test, but is instead continually developing and evolving. This is shown by the way that revolutionary or mould-breaking design idea, which get accepted, come to be seen as obvious in time. Thus, the quite notable modern, functional style of Burleigh was followed by many schools comprised of large-windowed, panelled, box-like buildings piled together along pathways and around courtyards. As a result, it is quite hard to appreciate, now, the way Burleigh must have appeared to observers in the late 1940s. As has been discussed, there are signs that appreciations of Woodlea are similarly developing, as more school buildings come to include the energy-efficient features that seemed quite singular when Woodlea was designed and built.

Considering these notable schools has demonstrated how changes in educational, as well architectural, ideas influence the continued evaluation of a school building. As has been discussed, the initial design of a school building is partly a product of the educational assumptions of the time, and this is very clearly shown by the development of open-plan primary schools. The comments of the recent head teachers at the schools studied demonstrate how evaluation of their design continues to evolve according to changes in educational ideas and practice. At Finmere, the features designed for small group and individual learning, such as the bays within the classroom, are causing problems now that more whole class teaching is favoured in primary schools. In contrast, Burleigh's more traditional, self-contained classrooms are not currently causing such difficulties, but were presumably less appropriate through the 1960s and '70s to the styles of teaching then being advocated.

It must then be expected in the case of new schools that evaluations of their designs from both architectural and educational perspectives will change over time. Perhaps some contemporary design features, notable in the first BSF schools, such as atrium entrances, will come to seem so obvious as not to appear worth evaluating. There might also be problems with particular aspects, that come to light over time, becoming irritating in their repetition, such as occurred with the tendency for post-war flat roofs to leak. Meanwhile, organisational features, such as multi-purpose social, work and circulation space, are likely to be continually re-evaluated and vary in their perceived usefulness depending in part on the assumptions and practices common within education at particular times.

Where do we go from here?

This chapter has looked at a number of UK schools, noted for their design, and considered the changing perceptions and experiences of their users. We have seen how societal factors, and specific ideas from education and architecture, influence original designs and then continue to affect reactions to the school. But what does this tell us about the prospects for the school currently being built down the road? What suggestions does this provide for the school communities now engaged in re-design?

It seemed worth asking whether this consideration of particular, notable schools might reveal some commonalities or general principles, which could be useful to those currently engaged with designing schools. It has been argued that although investigation of these schools does not reveal a single solution to school design, there are strong suggestions of aspects of the process of designing, building and using a school which should be considered. These can be understood as gaining and sustaining local community recognition of the school's intentions, as reflected in its design; constructing a building based on ambitious design values and attention to detail; and recognising that evaluation is a continually evolving process.

How this might be done in practice will form the bulk of this book. First, however, it is necessary to investigate the building blocks of the physical environment, the particular features that we might want to include in a new or refurbished school. What evidence is there about what works? Which elements offer value for money? These are the sorts of questions that we might expect to be answered by looking at research evidence, investigations of specific parts of a school building, rather than trying to understand the school as a whole in its community and historical context. As we shall discover in the next chapter, however, such simplification may be appealing, but it is far from straightforward.

2 The problems of poor environments for learning

What harm can be done by an inadequate school building?

Instinctively people tend to feel that a poor physical environment will have a detrimental effect on the activities that take place there, and that therefore a badly maintained or poorly designed school must have an impact on learning. Indeed it seems obvious that in a rundown school, staff and students will tend to feel less valued and motivated, leading to more absence from school, poor behaviour and ultimately lower academic achievement. We can probably all think of schools we have come across that fit this description, at least partially.

As we will explore in this chapter, there is research evidence for associations of poor school premises with these problems, suggesting how bad buildings could affect learning. Research shows that both teachers and learners notice the physical environment and develop opinions about it, recognising failings and short-comings (Cohen and Trostle, 1990; Maxwell 2000; Burke and Grosvenor, 2003). These feelings about the premises will influence their attitudes and views relating to the educational experience as a whole. This presumably affects behaviour in school (Kumar *et al.*, 2008; Rudd *et al.*, 2008), leads to impacts on the morale of students and staff (Hallam, 1996), and may influence attendance levels (Durán-Narucki, 2008). It has been argued these could be routes by which the physical environment could ultimately produce changes in students' academic achievement (Weinstein, 1979), contributing to the association that has been found between a neglected or deficient physical environment and achievement (Woolner *et al.*, 2007a).

We should be cautious, however, about accepting too readily a straightforward causal link between poor buildings and poor attainment. Although the possible mediating elements highlighted above, such as staff and student attitudes, attendance and behaviour, appear to demonstrate how such a causal relationship might work, they should also warn us of the complexity of the situation. Although suggestive, much of the research conducted in this area is broadly correlational, demonstrating associations between poor environment and learning, rather than clearly showing bad school buildings affecting learning. It seems possible that within the complex network of social, cultural and physical aspects of the school, the poor environment could be at least partly the result of other problems – an effect not a cause – though it might then contribute to further decline. For instance, a school where behaviour is poor may have difficulty maintaining a pleasant, welcoming and well-maintained environment in the face of vandalism and other damage. Conversely, a school where staff and student morale is high, with good standards of behaviour, might be able to make the most of an average, or even inadequate, building, finding ways to work successfully within its limits. A good description of this sort of relationship between premises and education is contained in the classic 'Fifteen thousand hours: secondary schools and their effects on children' (Rutter *et al.*, 1979). 12 secondary schools were studied in detail in an effort to assess the impact of the various elements of the total learning environment on the students. Considering the effect of the school premises, the authors comment that: 'the schools varied greatly in how they responded to the physical conditions available to them ... some of the older buildings had been made pleasant and attractive places ... other schools, by contrast, had done little to transform their surroundings' (p. 101).

It begins to look then as though there might be generally under-performing schools, which are inadequate in all sorts of ways, including having poor premises. If this is the case, a cynic might ask whether it is worth spending huge amounts of money constructing shiny new buildings for these schools, partly in the hope of improving learning and raising achievement. A possible answer to this has been most clearly articulated by commentators, activists and some researchers in the USA. They point out that although poor school premises are associated with a myriad of other social, cultural and economic disadvantages, the buildings themselves are an element which can be improved in a relatively straightforward manner, while the other problems might be more difficult to address directly. Given this, and the tendency for poor school buildings to co-occur with other disadvantage, these writers argue that there is a moral or social duty to try to sort out inadequate physical learning environments:

> The condition of school buildings is not randomly assigned. Poor, minority children are more likely to attend schools in disrepair. If school building condition is important . . . then the amelioration of school buildings could be a very simple way in which their education can be improved.
>
> Durán-Narucki 2008: 285

> The socio-economic status of students, the most important external factor in learning, cannot be controlled. Time in learning, the most direct internal factor can be controlled. Because the physical environment has an important influence on time in learning, and on other indirect, but significant factors in the learning process, policymakers should consider a building-based change process for school improvement.
>
> Young *et al.*, (2003: 2)

Problems and priorities: which aspects of a poor environment cause which consequences?

It has been argued in the previous section that poor school premises seem to be associated with poor outcomes and that, even if this relationship is not simple, there are likely to be benefits to improving an inadequate environment. This does not give much guidance, however, in how to address the problem since it does not show which aspects should be prioritised for improvement or the likely consequences of leaving certain elements as they are. For some ideas about this, we now turn to the research base to see what research evidence there is for the various categories of physical problems having an impact on health, attitudes, behaviour and attainment.

The following sections are based on a review carried out by the Reseach Centre for Learning and Teaching at Newcastle University on behalf of the Design Council and CfBT, two British charitable bodies that are involved in the current efforts at school regeneration. The results were subsequently published in an academic journal (Woolner *et al.*, 2007a) and the conclusions that we reached formed an important part of the review conducted as part of the first annual report from the evaluators of BSF (PricewaterhouseCoopers, 2007).

The original review process was intended to provide a synthesis of existing knowledge in a complex field, drawing on a number of disciplines, from the purely educational, to psychology, environmental and buildings design and ergonomics, with a variety of paradigms for research and reporting. Databases were searched, using relevant search terms, which produced a large number of books, journal articles and other material, of which over 200 were studied in depth. We found that despite general interest in some aspects of learning environments, there is frequently a paucity of clear, replicable empirical studies. There is a particular difficulty in finding research which addresses specific elements of the environment, and, where this exists, there has been more research into some aspects than into others. Interesting case studies have been reported, but there are issues of how replicable or generalisable these findings are. On the other hand, the most extensive studies are frequently based on correlations and associations, which, as has been discussed above, may be suggestive, but often fall short of demonstrating a causal relationship between buildings and learning.

Noise

Educationalist Julia Flutter has spent more than a decade involved in projects where students are consulted about their learning and has found that learners are concerned about their physical school environment, with a central worry being excessive noise:

'Noise and distracting behaviour were the most frequently mentioned problems and many students said they would like a calmer and quieter environment' (Flutter, 2006: 184). In schools awaiting BSF rebuilding work, problems with acoustics are considered by over three-quarters of head teachers to be affecting to 'a large extent' or 'to some extent' the school's provision of education (PricewaterhouseCoopers, 2008: 65). These findings show that noise or poor acoustics in schools are experienced as difficulties by both learners and staff. It must be questioned, however, what evidence there is for noise directly affecting learning as opposed to irritating teachers and learners.

There is in fact considerable literature considering the effect of noise on human functioning, quite a lot of it relating to children learning in noisy environments. Unusually for research into the impact of environmental factors on learning, in this area of noise research it is possible to find both laboratory and world-based studies, with conclusions which may be related to each other. Given these consistencies in the findings of field and laboratory approaches, some researchers have argued that it would be beneficial for studies to combine methodologies when considering the effect of raised levels of ambient noise on children (Cohen *et al.*, 1980).

The laboratory-based cognitive psychology experiments attempted to understand the effect of noise on cognitive functioning through examining impacts on the performance of narrow tasks, often involving memory (eg, Salame & Wittershiem, 1978). Although these produced good evidence that noise affects performance negatively, it is not clear how these problems are caused or whether they are always caused in the same way. Even these experiments, in situations which are considerably more restricted than in a classroom, allow for some argument about the precise cognitive mechanisms for the results they obtained (Poulton, 1978). This incomplete understanding makes it more difficult to suggest ways to cope with noise or anticipate when noise will be most problematic.

These laboratory experiments do, however, suggest explanatory elements that recur in the 'real world' literature. This includes noise annoyance, distraction and direct masking of cognitive processes, as well as revealing a general tendency for noise to be disruptive, therefore impairing performance. The 'real world' research into the effect of living or learning in noisy surroundings was initially driven by concerns about people's exposure to chronic external noise, such as that due to aircraft or road traffic. A review of the area discussed the possibility of health and psychological problems and concluded that: 'The evidence for effects of environmental noise on health is strongest for annoyance, sleep and cognitive performance in adults and children' (Stansfeld & Matheson, 2003: 253). A reliable finding is that chronic noise exposure impairs cognitive functioning, and a number of studies have discovered noise-related reading problems (Haines *et al.*, 2001b; Evans & Maxwell, 1997), deficiencies in pre-reading skills (Maxwell & Evans, 2000) and more general cognitive deficits (Lercher *et al.*, 2003).

Given the uncertainty, discussed above, about the mechanism through which noise affects cognitive processes, it is not surprising that there has been some discussion about the reason for the reliable reading deficits. It has been observed that teachers pausing during bursts of external noise leads effectively to a reduction in teaching time (Weinstein, 1979), which has been put as high as an 11 per cent loss in teaching time (Rivlin & Weinstein, 1984). 'Noise annoyance' and links to mood might be of practical concern if your surroundings are noisy (Boman & Enmarker, 2004; Kjellberg *et al.*, 1996; Lundquist *et al.*, 2002,2003). Importantly, however, there also seems to be a more direct cognitive mechanism (Haines *et al.*, 2001a).) A study which used recordings of aeroplanes, road traffic and trains found that these various noises appear to interfere with the encoding stage of memory (Hygge, 2003). This interference did not seem to be mediated by distraction or mood, so deficits in performance might be found even when a person does not feel upset or distracted by the noise. Other researchers in this area have argued that the reading deficits found in children in noisy surroundings result from problems with language acquisition and, specifically, with speech perception (Evans and Maxwell, 1997). This is consistent with the suggestion, based on laboratory and field studies, that impairment in performance is partly explained by the interference of any noise with inner speech (Poulton, 1978). Related to this, it appears that irrelevant speech is a particularly distracting noise (Knez and Hygge, 2002).

This evidence for noise interfering with thinking fuels concern about noise levels in schools, even where there are not excessively high levels of noise due to a motorway or flight path. Some research has considered ambient noise levels in British classrooms, where there is not particularly loud external noise. Shield and Dockrell (2004) found that external noise levels did not generally affect levels of classroom noise, which were mainly dependent on internal factors such as the nature of the classroom activity and the number of children. It must be noted, though, that this study measured the noise levels with the classroom windows closed, therefore generally reducing the measured extent of the external noise, and also departing from normal classroom conditions. Even so, when the children were engaged in silent reading, this study found that the external noises became more significant and possibly distracting. Furthermore, it was also found that background noise in unoccupied classrooms was above guideline levels, implying that normal ambient noise in the average school building might be problematic.

Other researchers have also drawn attention to problems of inadequate acoustics in schools (Addison *et al.*, 1999; Lundquist *et al.*, 2002) and various solutions have been proposed by those working in this area, including increased carpeting (Tanner & Langford, 2002), sound amplification systems (McSporran *et al.*, 1997) and ceiling hangings to dampen reverberation (Maxwell & Evans, 2000). As a demonstration of how some environmental issues in schools don't change, it's worth noting that this last solution was in use in the 1830s to reduce noise levels in large single-room schools (see Seaborne, 1971, plate 120 for details).

The conclusions that can be drawn from all this research are quite clear but do not prescribe school design solutions. There is plenty of evidence that noise has a direct impact on certain thought processes, as well as being possibly annoying or distracting. These direct effects on some parts of language processing would seem particularly serious for young children, and are probably the cause of deficits in reading which result from living or learning in places where there is excessive noise. This implies that it is important to consider the location of schools, particularly primary schools and nurseries, avoiding positioning them near busy roads if possible. Where a school is close to a noise source there is a need to measure noise levels around the site and perhaps put acoustic blocking features in place in the noise 'hot spots'. These might include landscaping or fencing outside, and perhaps thicker glazing for certain classrooms, although the need to open windows must not be forgotten.

Better acoustic division between classrooms might be helpful, in not allowing noise from other rooms to add to the noise coming from outside, since research measuring levels of internal noise has pointed out that such noise can be quite noticeable. Better acoustic separation between rooms in the school might include thicker walls and heavier glazing for any internal windows. Also the problem of noise seeping between rooms is reduced if the walls connect with the skeletal ceiling instead of a space being left for cabling behind a hanging, false ceiling. Such detailing may be beyond the scope of a refurbishment and will, of course, add to the cost of a school rebuild, so may be ruled impossible. In such cases, it might be worth examining whether organisational changes within school, such as explicitly timetabling noisy and quiet periods in the day, could reduce the impact of the noise on learners.

Air quality

There would seem to be fairly reliable evidence for poor air quality having an impact on general health and also on learning. Laboratory studies have shown how air quality can affect attention and concentration, suggesting problems likely to be caused by low air quality in classrooms. In reviews and reports that attempt to prioritise the elements of the physical environment where there is most evidence of an impact on learning, air quality is generally mentioned (see Young *et al.*, 2003; Buckley *et al.*, 2004; Earthman 2004, Fisher 2001). For example, the American educational administrator and planner Glen Earthman (2004) rated temperature, heating and air quality as the most important individual elements for student achievement. As part of a detailed review of the available evidence carried out for the Australian government in 2001, Kenn Fisher similarly rated these factors as likely to affect student behaviour and outcomes (Fisher, 2001). Showing how this might work in practice, there is a well-reported school renovation project, where the renovation of a very rundown elementary school in the USA led to increases in attendance and standardised test results, and the repair of the heating and ventilation system was a central part of the environmental improvements that were carried out (Berry, 2002).

Generally, the importance of ventilation in educational establishments is frequently emphasised (Kimmel *et al.*, 2000; Khattar *et al.*, 2003), while the inadequacies of indoor air in schools continue to be reported (Kimmel *et al.*, 2000; Khattar *et al.*, 2003) and linked to ill-health (Ahman *et al.*, 2000). Poorer health may impact on learning, partly through increasing absence and reducing available learning time. Particular links have been made between air quality and childhood asthma, resulting in some recommendations for school premises. Working in this area, researchers Smedje and Norback (2001) argued that since irritants and allergens collect in dust, it might be advisable to avoid particular sorts of 'fleecy' furnishings and open shelving and to increase the frequency of cleaning. It is evident that such concerns for clean air might come into conflict with a teacher's desire to provide a comfortable, cosy and welcoming classroom, in which resources are readily available to independent, active learners. This issue of evidence-based requirements relating to some aspects of the environment coming into conflict with other needs or recommendations will be addressed more fully in Chapter 3.

Most of the studies of school or classroom air quality assume that air-related health problems are self-evidently problematic, but the carefully constructed study of Rosen and Richardson (1999) went further by linking poor air quality to levels of attendance. They found that reducing the number of particles in the air – and so improving air quality – in a nursery school resulted in reduced child absence, which clearly would have implications for learning and academic achievement. In contrast, the Heschong Mahone Group (2003) reported that operable windows and air conditioning had no effect on school attendance. However, this apparent contradiction could be an instance of trying to reconcile a study of rectifying a poor environment, in the nursery school, with attempts to improve upon an adequate environment in the schools. If the air quality was already at an acceptable level in most of the schools, it would not be expected that further improvement would necessarily have an impact on absence from school.

Space

In Chapter 1, it was observed that the larger open-plan primary school, Eveline Lowe School, seemed to have been more successful than schools of a similar design. Given that it was more spacious than other open plan schools, it was suggested that this factor might be important. Certainly, during the 1970s, when open plan designs were being assessed, evaluations often referred to the necessity of adequate space. A detailed research study of open plan primary schools carried out at this time concluded that overcrowding was often a problem (Bennett *et al.*, 1980). The NUT report into open-plan schools published a few years earlier, when school numbers were particularly high, made this point about space quite forcefully. A teacher responding to their survey stated: 'There can be no movement or activity on any scale where there is no room to move' (NUT (England), 1974: 29). In addition to these direct problems with lack of space, a more crowded classroom or school is also likely to be noisier and more difficult to ventilate, problems which, as described above, can in themselves interfere with learning. So there are a number of reasons for considering the impact of reduced space on education.

As school rolls in the UK contracted, however, during the 1980s, this aspect of the educational setting received less attention. A notable exception to this was a small, but carefully conducted, piece of research which attempted to compare the attitudes of learners in two spacious primary classrooms with those in two cramped classrooms, where the space per pupil was considerably less (Clift *et al.*, 1984). The questionnaire which was used measures attitudes to learning and school, and produces separate ratings for ten aspects, such as 'interest in school work' and 'attitude to class'. These range from quite personal elements of self concept relevant to learning, through attitudes to the teacher and the class, to more global attitudes to school. When the scores on these scales were compared across the four classes, an interesting pattern emerged, with statistically significant differences being found for some scales between the cramped and spacious classrooms. These were the scales relating to relationships and attitudes within the classroom and class group, while the more personal and the more global attitudes to learning tended not to conform to this pattern. Thus, this small scale study reveals an association of classroom space with learner attitudes and perceptions relating to the teacher and class group. This suggests that the space available in the classroom might have a fairly direct impact on the attitudes and social relationships of students, which we might expect to affect their learning.

The authors of this study concluded that their results were 'necessarily tentative' (*ibid.*: 212) and that further, larger scale, research projects were needed. Yet, as described above, decreasing school populations led to this issue seeming a less pressing concern. So there have been no concerted efforts to try to understand the details of the apparent relationship. The students studied by Clift and colleagues were in their final year of primary school, and it is hard to judge what the impact of restricted space might be on younger and older learners. Adequate space seems likely to be more important for younger children, whose learning activities might be more active, but older children will of course be bigger and make a given area seem smaller. It is also unclear how this issue translates to secondary school, where students use a number of rooms, and where different subjects may have differing needs for space.

The likely impact of restricted space on aspects such as student attitudes and actual classroom practice continues to be mentioned, however, if not rigorously researched. For example, architect Sandra Horne-Martin includes student density in her recent overview of the elements of the physical school environment which affect learning (Horne-Martin, 2006: 99). She is also convinced, however, of the importance of how a teacher organises and uses the space available. It seems probable that while thoughtful organisation will be unable to compensate for a really restricted or overcrowded space, in many more average classrooms, careful arrangement of furniture and equipment might make a difference. A recent study of the use of carpet space in primary classrooms (McCarter, 2009) found that restricted space led to student discomfort. Yet this had been overcome in one classroom studied through arranging the furniture to maximise the carpet space. In their book about classroom organisation of materials and equipment, Loughlin and Suina propose that the arrangement and positioning of material is a 'tool to support the learning process' (1982: xv). They argue that the methods used to store and arrange equipment affect how, and whether, items get used and are returned afterwards. Further ideas for alterations and improvements which can be made within classrooms, and which may facilitate learning providing that the basic area available is adequate, will be considered in later chapters.

Temperature

Research findings relating to problems of learning in uncomfortable temperatures tend to be entangled with issues of ventilation and air quality. Often reviews consider the implications for 'HVAC' – heating, ventilation and air conditioning systems. Furthermore, many of the background assumptions and foundational ideas about temperature control tend to come from the USA and we might question whether any effects on learning will translate to schools in a more moderate climate such as that of the UK. It is also worth pointing out that where mechanical methods of heating or cooling are proposed, this is likely to conflict with desires for a quiet learning environment, since air conditioning, ventilation and heating systems have been found to contribute quite distinctly to the level of classroom noise (Shield & Dockrell, 2004).

There is, however, a consistent body of evidence suggesting that problems are experienced with temperatures in British schools, as well as in other buildings. Studies of user perceptions within workplaces have shown that 'thermal comfort is still close to the top of the list of chronic complaints' (Leaman & Bordass, 2001: 133). In schools awaiting redesign through BSF issues with heating and cooling are often considered by staff to be having a negative impact on education. The second evaluation of BSF reports survey findings to this effect and quotes a deputy head teacher who complained that 'classrooms are ... hot in the winter and cold in the summer' (PricewaterhouseCoopers, 2008: 65). In her assessment of the aspects of the school environment that will impact on learning, Horne-Martin highlights temperature. She illustrates this point with a photograph of a classroom where the temperature was only 7°C resulting in 'lack of attention and "fidgeting"' (Horne-Martin, 2006: 98).

These experiences and findings concur with the frustrations voiced by teachers we have worked with as part of a participatory design process, and with comments made by teachers, students and other school users I have met. Especially in schools built during the post-war period, with their big windows and relatively light-weight construction, it is very common for users to complain that they are too hot during the summer and cold in the winter. As a teacher in a 1970s built primary school included in an energy survey complained, it is often an experience of 'freezing in winter and boiling in summer' (Bunn, 2008). The annoyance of these school users seems to be as much to do with their lack of control over these conditions as with the absolute temperatures, although the dramatic seasonal variations clearly exacerbate the situation. In fact, there is more general evidence from surveying users in a range of buildings which suggests that the essential problem with indoor temperatures is lack of control over them. The survey referred to above argues that 'it is vital to give occupants power of intervention to control, override or at least trade-off some of the main heating, cooling, ventilation, lighting and noise parameters' (Leaman & Bordass, 2001: 133). A survey of recently constructed, energy efficient, schools also concluded that user control of heating and cooling are central to user satisfaction with the physical environment (DfES, 2006).

Lighting

Architects and designers tend to be convinced of the necessity of good lighting, with as much natural light as possible. While this might seem sensible, it is difficult to find research evidence for problems caused directly by dingy rooms. There is some evidence that lighting affects mood and attitude, which might then influence performance (Knez, 1995). Veitch (1997) however, argued that lighting has no effect on mood or performance, while Knez (2001) found that females were more perceptive to light than males, with males and females performing differently in different kinds of lighting. In terms of attendance and wellbeing, the Heschong Mahone Group (2003) asserted that physical classroom characteristics, including lighting, do not affect student attendance, but other researchers, for example Hathaway (1994), suggest that there is a correlation between absenteeism and lighting.

Somewhat more evidence does exist for poorly designed lighting causing problems in the area of environmental research concerned with health issues such as headaches, eyestrain and fatigue. These sorts of complaints seem to be exacerbated by inadequate lighting or poor shielding from glare associated with the use of ICT, particularly personal computers and interactive whiteboards (IWBs). With the increased use of computers and other ICT in schools, the idea of creating glare free lighting is important (Barnitt, 2003), and some studies advocate the use of full spectrum polarised lighting, as it is glare free and flicker free (Karpen, 1993).

It might be, however, that there is no neat solution to the competing demands made on lighting in schools. A review of the impact of lighting drew attention to the difficulty of deciding whether the focus should be upon luminosity or chromatic distinction, to give but two of many factors, and recommended: 'As a practical matter, ergonomists, along with lighting designers, architects, facilities managers and other lighting specifiers, should end their search for the ideal fluorescent lamp for all circumstances....

[C]hoices should be made with an eye to their suitability for the task, the building, the local culture, and the lighting system performance, including energy efficiency and aesthetic judgements' (Veitch & McColl, 2001: 274). If this recommendation is accepted when a school is being redesigned, it implies an inclusive approach to the planning of lighting. This should include consideration of the many different lighting needs across the various parts of the school, together with the preferences and priorities of the users of these spaces. As with temperature, it seems likely that control will be important to users, and good controls will also allow more flexibility to produce lighting that is appropriate to particular tasks and activities.

Maintenance and renovation

Back in the 1950s a rather elaborate psychology experiment sat participants in either an 'ugly' room or a 'beautiful' room to carry out a highly artificial task, and compared the judgements they made about a set of photographs. The settings are lovingly described in the original research report (Maslow & Mintz 1956), and the researchers found that participants in the considerably less pleasant surroundings made significantly less positive judgements about the photographs. This provides experimental evidence of the general conviviality of surroundings affecting ideas formed about quite separate issues, and suggests how an unpleasant environment may taint the activity which takes place there.

Although this seems worrying for schools with less than ideal premises, it is necessary to question how much of a problem it appears to be in practice. Although it is straigtforward to find schools where the environment seems to be contributing to their problems, it is always possible to find schools that buck the trend. A recent comparative case study looking at sustainable schools found a primary school apparently maintaining staff morale, developing happy children and achieving very high academic standards, despite a crumbling, wholly inadequate building (Bunn, 2008).

A suggestion of the extent of the problem of generallly poor buildings is provided by a number of studies which have correlated measures of the quality of the physical environment in schools with outcomes such as standardised test results, attendance or the prevalence of troubling behaviour. An American study by an architect found that his judgments of the quality of school premises in a sample of 14 schools correlated positively with measures of student achievement, but within this study socio-economic differences between the schools were not correlated with achievement, which is unusual (Tanner, 2000). In the UK, a study published in 2000, found an association between capital expenditure on school infrastructure and student achievement, but it was far from clear which of these factors was cause and which was effect (PricewaterhouseCoopers, 2000).

Two recent American studies have worked very thoroughly with large data sets. One study used data from an entire school district, examining correlations of independent, pre-existing quantified judgments of school premises standards with test results (Duran-Narucki, 2008). The other study used a large representative sample of schools across the US and correlated ratings of premises with student reports of behaviour (Kumar *et al.*, 2008). Although the findings were quite complicated and not entirely conclusive, there was general evidence of an association of poor quality surroundings with troubling behaviour, truancy and lower test results. Of course these are only correlational, not causal, relationships, so our evaluation of these particular studies should be cautious, as discussed previously.

Taken together with the impact of the 'beautiful' and 'ugly' rooms on other judgments, however, this does begin to seem suggestive. If all other things are equal, which in reality they rarely are, a poor school environment seems likely to increase negative perceptions among staff and students, which would be expected to contribute to troublesome behaviour, truancy and lower achievement. A good test of this relationship in action would be to degrade a school building and look at the consequences, but this would hardly be ethical! We could, however, examine what happens in the contrasting situation when deficient premises are suddenly improved, through renovation or rebuilding.

Some research has explicitly attempted this, while some other studies which attempt to link school environments and learning more generally can be interpreted as evidence for the impact of renovation. An interesting case study, mentioned earlier in this chapter (Berry, 2002) describes the renovation of a rundown inner city school in the US, and includes measurements of attitude, behaviour and achievement taken before and after the renovation project. It is clear from the descriptions that the school premises were in considerable disrepair beforehand. After the renovation the study reports that the attitudes of all the school's users had improved, there was increased parental involvement, more extra-curricular activities and some evidence of an improvement in standardised test results. Seemingly the renovation had worked magic! However, it must be remembered that such renovation projects rarely appear from nowhere. The case study does not mention this project's antecedents, but it could be that attitudes were already beginning to change at the school and part of rising morale and expectations was organising a facelift for the building.

This is not to detract, though, from the positive effects that successful renovation of an inadequate or tired learning environment can have. In an American college in the 1970s, researchers found that a renovated teaching room, including soft furnishings and designed to be more friendly and attractive, seemed to increase student participation (Sommer & Olsen, 1980). They report that student participation rates in discussions and in asking questions during classes were 'two or three times as high' (*ibid.*: 13) as in comparable classes taught in traditional rooms. Closer to home, some of the initial outcomes of the current wave of school building work across the UK can be interpreted as demonstrating the power of renovation. A research survey (Estyn, 2007) of the schools in Wales which had at that time undergone rebuilding and refurbishment reported that achievement had quite consistently and significantly risen in the schools following the building work. There was also some evidence of a direct influence of school condition on the quality of teaching, with more lessons rated higher by Ofsted inspectors after renovation. This is interesting because it provides a plausible mechanism for the reported improvement in student achievement, and suggests the wider impact of school surroundings on all users. Yet the important detail that is not provided by this study is the condition of the schools before the rebuilding work. Despite the centrality of knowing the starting point for assessing the value of particular changes to the environment or comparing proposed improvements, this report, which makes the case for refurbishment affecting teaching and learning, does not engage with initial conditions. However, since the schools which received the investment were part of an ongoing programme across Wales to improve the stock of school buildings, it seems likely that this will be proceeding partly through prioritising and these first schools were considered to be in greater need. So it might be suggested that this survey, at this stage, provides good evidence of the benefits of improving inadequate schools rather than proving a simple causal relationship between premises and the learning which takes place there.

Similar reasoning can be applied to early reports from the BSF initiative in England of improved school buildings having impacts on student attitudes and behaviour (e.g. Rudd *et al.*, 2008), since the BSF programme has proceeded so far partly through prioritisation. Two questions then arise from these observations. Firstly, how long can the improved attitude and performance of both teachers and students in the schools already renovated be maintained? Secondly, as building programmes such as these proceed, will there be an inevitable fall off of demonstrable results? Both these questions require us to develop a better, more complete, understanding of the complexities of the relationship between school environments and their users, which goes beyond highlighting the immediate impact of the amelioration of distinct deficiencies. In particular it seems important to try to understand the effects of change in an already passable or fairly adequate setting. As mentioned previously, the research evidence for such impact is considerably weaker, more inconsistent and generally open to interpretation. Yet if we are to understand the likely trajectories of response to change within particular schools and across the stock as a whole, we need to engage with this evidence. Therefore it is research evidence relevant to, or explicitly addressing, this part of the relationship between environment and behaviour to which we turn in Chapter 3.

3 How much is enough? Trying to improve learning environments

Going beyond an 'adequate' environment to benefit education

As the evidence considered in the previous chapter demonstrates, there are good reasons for being concerned about education taking place in poor environments. It appears that the physical environment can adversely affect learning, sometimes through direct impacts on learning processes, sometimes through affecting health and wellbeing, as well as through causing frustration and irritation among teachers and learners. Evidence is also emerging for renewal or refurbishment leading to improvements in the attitudes and behaviour of teachers and learners, which can be linked to improved teaching and learning experiences, and, ultimately, to increases in attainment.

It was argued that these reported impacts of an improved learning environment might be best understood as further evidence of the problems of an inadequate environment. Yet the improvements made to these schools will have gone beyond merely bringing them up to adequate levels. This leads to questions about the point at which the educational returns on these expensive investments begin to diminish. Also, given that the money spent on a school might be large but will not be infinite, we should ask whether it is possible to identify priorities for that expenditure. Reaching some conclusions in this area is not idle speculation since governments repeatedly have to deal with stocks of schools where some are judged inadequate, and it is then necessary to agree how the capital available should be shared out. For example, in 1962, the publication of a detailed government survey into primary school buildings (DfES, 1962) revealed how many buildings were old and lacking basic facilities such as inside toilets, but could not tell the government of the time how to priorities spending. More recently as BSF began, it was reported that a quarter of secondary schools did not conform to existing standards and regulations (Ofsted, 2001). The difficulties associated with inadequate school premises would suggest that bringing these schools up to standard should be a priority, but should we aim to improve them further? In addition, how important is it for the three-quarters of schools fulfilling the basic standards to make some improvements?

In attempting to answer these questions, it is necessary to look at the rather more equivocal and mixed evidence relating to the assessment and alteration of learning environments where the setting does not seem to be fundamentally inadequate. It will also involve considering the implications of attempting to rectify some the problems indentified in the previous chapter. Furthermore, although much of the research into problem environments has investigated particular aspects of these environments in isolation, they actually exist together within the school. Attempting to improve the learning environment necessitates understanding any interactions or conflicts. In developing this understanding, it will become increasingly important to move beyond noting associations of physical features with teaching or learning outcomes to map out the complex relationships between the school environment and the people using it. Any outcomes from a change to the setting are likely to be produced through an involved chain of events, and defining these mediating chains is key.

Understanding the evidence for the effects of improvements

Differing opinions across the school community

One reason that it is difficult to answer questions about how much improvement is enough is revealed through considering the needs and desires of a range of school users. As might be expected, research tends to reveal differences of opinions between individuals. For example, there is enormous variation in preferences for different colours so even where designers suggest that certain colours are conducive to learning or more appropriate for particular ages of children, they do not always agree with each other. It is possible to read in one place that younger children prefer bright colours and patterns (Engelbrecht, 2003), while another writer suggests strong, warm colours for young children, warning specifically against the use of intense primary colours (Pile, 1997). One piece of experimental research asked participants to perform various tasks while seated in booths which were painted in the participant's preferred colour, and did suggest that learners perform better surrounded by their preferred colour (Bross & Jackson, 1981). However, since learners' colour preferences will vary widely, this is not a very useful result when considering what colour to paint a classroom.

Importantly, there seem to be some systematic differences between various groups within the school community in how they perceive the school environment. Researchers investigating learning environments have developed techniques, questions and rating scales to measure users' opinions and perceptions, sometimes as part of planning improvements to a school environment (e.g. Berry, 2002; Maxwell, 2000). Evidence has been collected both in the UK and in other countries, albeit for a variety of purposes and in various forms. This includes the opinions of teachers (Schapiro, 2001; Cooper, 1985), children (Burke & Grosvenor, 2003; Cohen & Trostle, 1990) and school principals (Tanner and Langford, 2002).

In an American elementary school, questionnaires given to students, staff and parent revealed that the adults were considerably more inclined than the children to perceive cleanliness and maintenance as important to the school seeming 'welcoming'. Meanwhile, the parents and the students were more likely than the staff to mention such aspects as the visitor policy, car parking and landscaping in making the school welcoming (Maxwell, 2000: 276–277). This study and others also reveal some commonalities, however, in the opinions of the various user groups within educational settings (Maxwell, 2000; Douglas & Gifford, 2001). The results of a consultation we carried out in a secondary school identified features of the school which students, teachers and other staff all agreed were serious problems, although there were clear differences in the salience and immediacy of particular deficiencies for the various users (Woolner *et al.*, 2010)

Some work shows that the priorities or main concerns of the various users of a school may differ (Fraser, 1984; Maxwell, 2000; Ornstein, 1997). An example of this is the suggestion of some research that children are more concerned than adults about colour around their school environment. In the American elementary school, mentioned above, the children thought colour was important and that the colour of the walls in their school was uninviting and boring, but the staff and parents did not share these concerns (Maxwell, 2000). British educationalists Cathy Burke and Ian Grosvenor further emphasise children's preference for colour. In their book, The School I'd Like (Burke & Grosvenor, 2003), a collection of student ideas about desirable school environments, many children mentioned colours or drew colourful pictures. One 15-year-old student described her school as 'a giant magnolia prison. I want colours'(p. 25).

Different users can also react differently or behave differently in response to particular parts of the environment. One study of preschool children found that ceiling height affected cooperative behaviour, with the children displaying higher levels of cooperative behaviour in classrooms with lower ceilings (Read *et al.*, 1999). However, another study found that higher ceilings in classrooms reduce perceptions by both teachers and children of crowding, with the height of the classroom ceiling correlating significantly with teacher satisfaction with the room (Ahrentzen & Evans, 1984). So, despite the desire to base designs on research evidence, there is no evidence-based ceiling height that will be universally suitable. It will be important for the school community to work with the architects and designers to produce ceilings with which they feel comfortable, perhaps of differing heights in different parts of the school, according to the purposes of the various spaces.

Even when users all seem to react in similar ways to a part of their environment, there may be differences between the user-groups in what they think should be done or the level to which an aspect must be improved. For example, in the American elementary school studied by Maxwell (2000) all the user groups who were asked agreed that displaying students' work made the school more welcoming. While the parents and teachers, however, thought that the school was doing this well, the students were less satisfied. If the perceptions of the school users were to be used as a guide for improvement work, this would raise, rather than solve, uncertainties about priorities.

Assessing value for money

As discussed above, the intention to base school designs on research evidence can lead to problems when evidence about the effects of a particular aspect of the environment is complicated or there appear to be differential effects across various groups of school users. The apparently sensible call to look at the relevant evidence can also produce difficulties when it is necessary to compare several possible improvements and try to judge which are most worth making. It is not enough to know that an impact on learning is likely, which is what the research might conclude. In the context of a decision about funding alterations to a school, it would be useful to have an idea of how great the improvement might be, in relation to the time, effort and money required to enact it, providing a way to compare the improvement with other changes to the school environment and organisation. As we concluded in 2005 from our review of the research then available, this is an aspect that research into learning environments does not generally address. So 'it is not possible on the basis of the available evidence to weigh the potential benefits of environmental improvements against alternative uses for these monies, such as professional development or the provision of teaching assistants. It would be useful if future research directly and explicitly addressed this issue of comparison and cost-benefit analysis' (Woolner *et al*, 2007a: 61).

Although this aspect of the impact of change to the learning environment still does not seem to be addressed explicitly in the research literature, it may be possible for schools or LAs to calculate costs relevant to their own situations and weigh these against expected benefits. These judgements will probably continue to be easier to make, however, within the area of physical improvements, rather than between physical and other changes. There is increasing research interest in the roles and experiences of support staff in schools, some of which addresses their impact on the behaviour and learning of students (Blatchford *et al*., 2007), but this is still a relatively new area in education research. It is currently revealing the complex nature of the support staff input rather than quantifying it.

Another aspect of the modern educational environment with distinct implications for spending decisions is the relative importance of technology. Research in this area, although more established than the study of support workers, also tends to investigate the teaching and learning possibilities of technological tools, as opposed to attempting to quantify their value or benefits. There is perhaps also a tendency to see new technology as an inherently good thing, with any querying of the usefulness of particular innovations identifying the questioner as a Luddite. This is evident in the early meetings arranged at LA level for school staff prior to BSF, when advice about ICT from representatives of multinational technology companies may be received surprisingly uncritically.

A notable exception to this attitude is found in the work of American educational researcher, Larry Cuban, who at the beginning of the new millennium, argued that schools were in danger of spending a lot of money on computers without properly considering what was useful in the classroom (Cuban, 2001). His research questions whether the utility of the educational technology embraced in the 1990s was proportional to its cost, and whether the most appropriate technologies were being adopted. Similar reservations were expressed by researchers in the UK during the early days of interactive whiteboards (IWBs), when it appeared that big sums of money were being committed without clear evidence of educational usefulness (Smith *et al.*, 2005).

In both these cases, the technologies are now more developed and better understood, allowing more balanced decisions to be made. Yet there is still a problem of enthusiasm about the teaching and learning potential of a new technology blinding us to the costs of implementing it, and causing us to overlook cheaper, 'lower-tech' alternatives. Teachers often assume that their students will be impressed or motivated by new ICT. Our evaluation of the Design Council's Schools Renaissance project did reveal that students using the technologically advanced 360° classroom tended to rate this technology as one of the positive aspects of the room. Their comments, however, also revealed that they were not over-whelmed and had some reservations, particular regarding technical problems with the equipment. Given the expense of equipping such a room, and keeping up with technological developments, we concluded that a learning space design centred on a complex of new technology was 'inherently risky' (Woolner *et al.*, 2007b).

Some of the studies which correlate aspects of the physical environment with positive outcomes for student learning or behaviour suggest that sometimes the advantages of the better environments may be due to relatively small differences in physical attributes. For example, some researchers argue that the effective display of student work increases feelings of ownership and involvement, leading to higher motivation (Killeen *et al.*, 2003; McGonigal, 1999). A correlational study which rated aspects of American schools and related them to student achievement provides suggestions for the broad elements of school design which might be particularly important for a successful learning environment (Tanner, 2000). Among the four features of the school design assessment scale which correlated with student achievement were 'pathways' and 'positive outdoor spaces'. The former refers to buildings and grounds which encourage ease of movement, presumably avoiding feelings of crowding. With reference to the latter factor, Tanner, an architect by training, was convinced of the benefit of well designed and maintained outdoor spaces and his findings imply a contribution to student academic performance. With both these aspects of the environment, the research is not prescriptive about exactly what counts as adequate pathways or outdoor spaces, and the ratings were based on subjective perceptions not measurements of area or light. This is not suggestive of a direct link to expenditure, and the research could be read as implying the benefit of simple, perhaps inexpensive, but well thought through designs for circulation and outdoor space.

Considering now research into changes to the physical environment, a similar central point emerges. This is the suggestion that some relatively inexpensive alterations can be as effective, or even more effective, than much more costly projects. Through the Design Council's Schools Renaissance project, alterations were designed and enacted in three secondary schools (Hall & Wall, 2006). The school that experienced the most far-reaching change made some apparently simple alterations to its communications strategy, through installing information screens, and remodelled the staff room. As these changes were made in the context of reflection and debate across the school staff about communication and organisation, they led to further re-evaluations and cycles of change. This resulted in a re-organisation of the school day, which was judged to have positive impacts on staff and students. In contrast, the apparently more ambitious, and expensive, 360° classroom built in another of the project schools, created many local difficulties but did not seem to impact more generally on the functioning of the school.

In the third school, designers attempted to address the problem of a narrow corridor by decorating it to seem wider and to discourage people from loitering. Observations suggested that this approach was surprisingly successful. Students in the school devised ways of measuring behaviour in the corridor, carried these methods out and concluded that behaviour had been improved by the redecoration. While the students' findings concur with the results of a study which compared a wide and a narrow corridor in a school (Ross, 2006), it is notable that the Schools Renaissance renovation was able to achieve a positive impact without expensive, and disruptive, rebuilding work.

Although there is clearly a need for a properly controlled study to compare such degrees of redesign, it seems undeniable that, in some circumstances, a cheaper or easier alteration to the learning environment might be as effective as a much more elaborate or expensive scheme. The deciding factor is likely to be the fit of the alteration, in terms of its costs as well as its potential benefits, to the wider aims and culture of the particular school. Yet again, this suggests understanding the perspectives of people from across the school community and building their involvement into the project as it develops.

Competing or conflicting areas for improvement

One problem that is not generally addressed in the more quantitative research into learning environments is the practical implications of attempting to improve a particular aspect of the physical environment. The challenges of prioritising elements of the environment may already seem large, given disagreements in users' perceptions and uncertainty about value for money, but it often seems to be assumed that these parts of the environment exist as independent building blocks, to be assessed and improved in isolation. In a school, however, these aspects will interact. Changing one part of the environment might impact on other aspects.

For example, given the findings relating noise to deficiencies in learning, it has been suggested that fabric ceiling hangings might be used to deaden echo noise and improve classroom acoustics (Maxwell & Evans, 2000). While this idea could achieve the primary aim, it may also decrease the air quality in the classroom, through increased dust and allergen particles being held in the fabrics. Other ideas for enhancing the learning experience could similarly have a negative impact on air quality. For instance, a book of suggestions for practical changes at the classroom level (Loughlin & Suina, 1982) argues that learning can be improved through accessible storage, with resources readily available to help learners develop independence, but having more open shelving is likely to lead to more dust accumulating. Even the suggestions often made about improving or increasing the display of students' work might lead to more dust. It is certainly worth considering whom on the school staff is going to be responsible for dusting and cleaning the elaborate tiled murals or other installations which are sometimes suggested as a way of improving student motivation (see e.g. Kileen *et al.*, 2003 for a description of an extensive tiled mural in a school).

The potential of solutions to noise problems to impact adversely on air quality are mirrored by the likelihood that trying to improve school air quality through ventilation will raise noise levels. Air conditioning, ventilation and heating systems are found to contribute quite distinctly to the level of classroom noise (Shield & Dockrell, 2004), while opening windows might also lead to noise problems in an urban school. Higher ceilings can also increase acoustic problems due to reverberation. Further, it has been argued that a particular problem with older schools is that their high ceilings 'may negate the benefit of better lighting' (Earthman, 2004: 20). Yet, as mentioned above, some research has found that higher ceilings in classrooms decrease perceptions of crowding, and increase teacher satisfaction (Ahrentzen and Evans, 1984). Therefore, although changing ceiling height could be proposed as a way to add value to an environment, it is still difficult to be certain, on the basis of the evidence, in which direction it should be altered. As argued above, a range of ceiling heights across the school constructed according to discussion about purposes and needs might be more appropriate than searching the research evidence for an ideal ceiling height.

The discussion of conflicts between the teacher's desire to create a comfortable, interesting classroom and the threat to air quality suggests the difficulty for the individual teacher of arranging their classroom to fulfil multiple aims. Clearly the conflicts for an educator trying to arrange a classroom to enhance learning extend beyond problems with air quality. Research suggests that the arrangement of furniture and equipment within the classroom makes a difference to learning, but the most appropriate arrangement will depend on what learning is intended to take place (see Figure 3.1).

Sandra Horne-Martin (2002; Horne, 1999), an architect who has carried out observational studies in classrooms, argues that style of teaching and room organisation are linked. Broadly, teachers who tend to teach in a more traditional didactic style are found in classrooms with a traditional arrangement of furniture, consisting of desks and chairs, usually in rows, all facing the front. In contrast, teachers who prefer to encourage group work or discussion as learning activities tend to occupy less traditional classrooms, perhaps through seating learners in groups or having more space for movement. However, it is not clear which is cause and which is effect. It seems likely that in some cases, teachers who value particular ways of learning will have rearranged their classrooms to facilitate these methods, while in other cases a classroom with a particular arrangement might have contributed to the ease or success of certain learning activities and encouraged the teacher to favour a particular way of working. But, of course, neither the arrangement of the classroom nor the teaching style of the teacher is static. Together with the two way direction of influence, this produces a complex relationship.

Looking for empirical evidence, some research into open plan learning environments has found that more open classrooms do have some direct effect on how teachers teach (Ahrentzen & Evans, 1984). However, other studies found that this was not as dramatic as might be expected: despite being encouraged by the policies of the school and the lay-out of the classroom to be more flexible and less traditional, many of the teachers stayed in one place, essentially 'taught from the front' and did not move the furniture (Rivlin and Rothenberg, 1976) . In general, as Weinstein and David pointed out, 'open-space, in and of itself, does not have a universal effect' (1987: 12) while Canter and Donald considered that in studies comparing open and traditional environments, 'the essential element was the school's educational philosophy and physical layout, not merely the physical layout on its own' (1987: 1292). Away from research on school environment, it has been found that open-plan offices do not necessarily change staff behaviour in the ways anticipated (Brennan *et al.*, 2002).

One of the more basic variables that can be altered in the classroom is the arrangement of the students' desks and chairs, and this narrow issue has been quite well researched and debated. Rows of desks are considered to be appropriate to individual work and increase time on task (Galton *et al.*, 1999). Research which specifically compared rows and tables suggests that less attentive and less successful pupils are particularly affected by the desk arrangement, with their on-task behaviour increasing very significantly

Figure 3.1 Classrooms showing teacher adjustments, within the constraints of an unusual 1980 open plan primary school.

when seated in rows instead of at tables (Wheldall *et al.*, 1981, Wheldall & Lam, 1987; Hastings, 1995). It is pointed out by these authors that the vital mediating element between the physical environment and improved classroom climate could be the reduction in negative interactions between teacher and student, since the student in the rows arrangement is able to concentrate and so provokes fewer admonishments.

Within the rows arrangement, there seem to be differences in student involvement dependent on position, with an 'action zone' of increased involvement across the front and down the middle of the room. There has been some discussion about whether this is more accurately characterised as a 'T' shape or as a triangle but there is agreement about the existence of such a zone. This pattern of student involvement is observed even with random allocation of seats, suggesting that it is not simply due to the more attentive students choosing to sit near the front (Weinstein, 1979; Gump, 1987). Moore *et al.*, (1984) found evidence that the differences in learner involvement found in different parts of the classroom originate in the questioning and attentiveness of the teacher rather than students' behaviour. This might have implications for whether students should have permanently assigned places or be encouraged to change places.

The discussion of differential student involvement when seated in rows and the findings that rows are particularly appropriate for individual work, suggests the importance of considering the purpose of the learning activities being attempted. Such classroom organisation will not be as appropriate for whole class discussions or group work, and may actually impede learning in these ways. Thus the aims and intentions of the teacher for some parts of the session may conflict with the classroom arrangement which has been chosen to support other learning. There would seem to be two alternative solutions to this problem. Either the furniture must be rearranged during the lesson or a compromise arrangement must be found. Many educationalists, on the basis mainly of teaching experience, recommend a 'horse shoe' formation where students can see each other and the teacher (Alexander, 1992; McNamara & Waugh, 1993; Galton *et al.*, 1999). Not so much research has been carried out on this arrangement compared to the investigations of rows, but it seems likely that a horse shoe would facilitate class discussion, as well as whole class teaching, and also support individual work without distractions. Although architect Sandra Horne-Martin (2002) argues this is a very controlling and teacher dominated approach, an educational study found that more questions were asked by children when seated in this arrangement rather than in rows (Marx *et al.*, 2000). A recent study of the use of space in classrooms in a British primary school found this desk arrangement being used successfully with a class of six to eight year old children (McCarter, 2009). Importantly, it left more floor free for an increased carpet space, which could then be used for a wider range of activities and was rated as considerably more comfortable by the learners.

This awareness of the physical comfort of learners brings us to the issue of ergonomic furniture. Ergonomic seating has been well researched in the workplace and there have been some studies in schools. A number of these have measured students and furniture, and demonstrated a mismatch between learners' body dimensions and the furniture they use (e.g Parcells *et al.*, 1999; Panagiotopoulou *et al.*, 2004). What is harder to find, however, is consistent evidence for an impact of more appropriate furniture on various measures of well-being, sitting positions or learning behaviour. Generally students express a preference for such furniture and experience it as more comfortable than traditional furniture. Given the differences in size between school children, some researchers have suggested that adjustable furniture might be sensible (e.g. Zandvliet & Straker, 2001). This is not a new idea: American school architect of the early twentieth century, John Donovan, includes a design for an adjustable desk and chair in his book of school architecture (Donovan, 1921). The failure of such ideas to become accepted in the UK is perhaps due to the possible conflicts between time spent adjusting the furniture and getting on with the lesson. This was indeed one of the problems experienced with prototype adjustable furniture designed for the 360° classroom during the Design Council's Schools Renaissance project (Hall & Wall, 2006; Woolner *et al.*, 2007b).

Trying to increase the time spent learning

The aspects of the learning environment considered in the previous section often appear to improve learning through increasing the opportunities for learning to occur. This might be through reducing the time spent managing disruptions by seating learners appropriately, or increasing the time in school by reducing ill-health and absence. This idea of the time spent learning being a vital mediating factor between the physical environment and student success or performance, has been advanced at various times to explain the possible impact of the environment on learning. For example, researchers who investigated the negative effect of high noise levels on reading hypothesised that the deficit might be the result of reduced learning time as teachers wait for quiet. As mentioned in the previous chapter, pausing by teachers during bursts of external noise produces an effective reduction in teaching time (Weinstein, 1979; Rivlin & Weinstein, 1984), which could contribute to the problems experienced by learners in noisy environments.

This idea of paying attention to the time available for learning makes intuitive sense and might provide a possible solution to the challenges outlined above of judging, and comparing, value for money in connection with the learning environment. It would certainly seem to be a sensible place for assessments at the school level to begin and perhaps provide an aspect of the learning environment which could be measured and compared as an alteration to the setting is put in place and evaluated. However, it seems important not to become too committed to such a narrow quantification of the school environment. Although learning might not be possible without some basic conditions, such as time being available, it is clear that these factors might be generally necessary but not sufficient for successful learning. It is important for learners to attend school or complete coursework, but there will be qualitative differences between learners who all achieve these first steps in how successful they are. Similarly, there must be qualitative, as well as quantitative, differences in learning experiences or opportunities, which may be affected by changes to the physical environment.

Ownership and involvement

Emerging from the research evidence relating to the impact of the physical environment on learning is a sense that it is hard to make generalisations about how the setting can most effectively facilitate the range of learning, teaching and social interactions that constitute school life. This would tend to concur with everyday experience in schools. Visiting schools reveals the differing organisations of people and premises; the surprisingly idiosyncratic solutions to local needs. Taken together, the research base and experience in schools suggests that once redesign work has addressed a school's distinct physical deficiencies, the next steps will depend on more individual priorities. Establishing the details of such needs and desires across the varied community of a school will perhaps be quite a lengthy task, which will be considered in more detail in the following chapters. A central benefit, however, is that any involvement of school users in the design process will tend to increase their sense of ownership of the resulting environment.

The positive effect of ownership is never really tested in research in this area, but assumptions about its importance underpin the ideas and methods of both educationalists and architects. It is only possible to make sense of many of the claims for the benefits of small scale innovations if implicit appeals to the importance of ownership are accepted. For example, participatory art projects might result in a mural or mosaic, but it is never claimed that any changes in attitude or satisfaction with the environment are due purely to the aethetic appeal of the art. Conversely, educational innovations that fail to become embedded elements of the practice of a school or teacher will tend to fade away. This is an established challenge to any attempts to 'roll out' small, successful ideas beyond their immediate proponents. Thus the literatures of both design and education reveal a need for ownership as an explanatory variable, even if the details of the ideas encompassed by this term are not completely understood.

Therefore, the idea of ownership as a foundation for the investigation or development of an educational setting arises both from the discovery that research evidence does not reveal an ideal learning environment, and from common practice in education and participatory design. It seems important, however, to look beyond this acceptance of ownership as a good idea, and to question just how it might be developed in the context of school design. This necessitates some form of participation of the school community in the design process. It is the detailed consideration of what this involves which will be the subject of the next two chapters.

4 The rationale for a collaborative design process

Introduction

Recently in the UK there has been an increase in enthusiasm for democratising education, specifically through more active involvement of learners. The interest in student or pupil 'voice' has been variously linked to international legislation on children's rights (United Nations Convention on the Rights of the Child, 1989) and the inclusion of citizenship in the British National Curriculum (Fielding, 2001a). It is notable, however, for being evident in practice in schools (in, for example, the resurgence of interest in school councils), within policy at both local and national level (e.g. Brighton & Hove City Council, 2003) and as a key element to current theorising and research about education (Thomson, 2008; Todd, 2007; Clark, 2004). Therefore there is a sense of inevitability about widespread encouragement to make contemporary school-building projects more inclusive and participatory. The question, then, is whether this represents fairly superficial linking to a fashionable trend or is an ambition that deserves to be taken more seriously.

I think there is considerable evidence that the involvement of people, both adults and children from across the school, and wider, communities is a necessary part of any school building or redesign project. It was noted in Chapter 1 that a contributory factor in continued satisfaction with a school appeared to be the engagement of the local community which provides current and potential users of the premises. Furthermore, as we have see in Chapters 2 and 3, there appear to be no complete answers to what constitutes an ideal learning environment. This suggests that involving learners, teachers and others in a discussion about current, future and desired usage should be enlightening and lead to a more appropriate design. Considering such involvement should also remind us that the process of designing and building a school will anyway involve a range of people from differing backgrounds. Even without a wide-ranging plan of participation, it will be a partnership of education professionals with architecture, design and construction professionals. The differing viewpoints and assumptions involved should warn us of the challenges of such partnership working. They also suggest, however, that the process might as well be yet more inclusive, involving learners, parents, non-teaching staff and the wider community. These people might not fit so snugly into either the education or architecture 'camps', but could offer different ideas again. Finally, as a reason for a collaborative design process, it must be remembered that some sort of involvement of users is generally a statutory duty with public building projects. A duty of consultation is part of BSF (DfES, 2002: 63). There is no ring-fenced money,however, and we will be returning to question how much, or how little, genuine partnership might be included in any consultation, especially where there are financial constraints.

It seems, therefore, that there might be good reasons for attempting some sort of participatory design process when building, rebuilding or modifying a school. This chapter will examine these in more detail, considering how they should be understood in the context of current, educational interest in 'voice', and through other frameworks for understanding participation. This appreciation of the potential of collaborative school design will then form the backdrop to the following chapter where we investigate how it might be done well in practice.

The potential benefits of participatory design

Benefits for the building

It seems self-evident that planners and architects designing any building would benefit from considering in some detail the purpose and intended use of the space. This leads to the idea that some involvement of the potential users in the design process should lead to more appropriate, closer fitting premises. The wider participation ensures that designers have access to user knowledge and experience, but should also set up relationships and understandings, providing the collaboration is long enough and valued sufficiently. This reasoning has underpinned the development of participatory planning, particularly urban planning, since the 1960s in Europe and the USA, and is becoming more influential in architecture (see Blundell Jones *et al.*, 2005). Some of those working in these fields have specifically argued that differences between lay and expert opinions about architecture mean that it is necessary to involve ordinary users in any design process (Till, 2005; Aspire *et al.*, 1981; Moore, 1979).

Architects and designers working in educational settings are of course influenced by these general trends, but there is also a particular historic relationship between architecture and education, which provides some clues about likely outcomes for school buildings that are designed collaboratively. Many writers have argued that during the nineteenth century's huge wave of school building architects were more concerned with society's general aims and ideals for mass education than with specifics of pedagogy or educational practice. So, for example, Markus (1996) notes analogies which likened the monitor-based schooling to factories and steam engines, and a number of writers have commented on the assumptions underlying the design of nineteenth century schools to facilitate constant surveillance (Markus, 1996; Lawn, 1999; Dudek, 2000). Seaborne and Lowe also point out that 'the view was widely held, although less often articulated, that the school building should contribute to the aesthetic sensibility of the child by showing him standards beyond those of his home' (1977: 4). Yet by 1911, Derbyshire school architect, Philip Robson was complaining that 'Architects generally regard schools as the easiest buildings to plan, and much difficulty arises from the fact that architects will not take the trouble to understand the educational side of the case' (Robson, 1911: 15). He, and others at the turn of the twentieth century, were beginning to be concerned with the detail of the relationship of their buildings to the educational activities that took place there. The idea was growing that architecture, through engaging with educational aims, could assist and positively influence these processes. This engagement with ideas and practice was not generally conceived as involving engagement with the teachers and learners themselves, however. As late as the 1930s, the award-winning school architect Denis Clarke Hall based his school designs on meticulous observations of school users but does not seem to have sought their interpretations or understandings of the processes they were involved in (Maclure, 1985: 7).

It was during the post war waves of school-building that the collaboration between architects and educationalists really developed, taking off during the immediate post war reconstruction of the 1940s and 1950s, becoming embedded by the 1960s-70s school building boom. The post war culture of collective and interdisciplinary ways of working nurtured successful relationships between educationalists and architects, who were generally working within local authorities or at central government level. These partnerships produced schools within tight physical constraints, that seemed to satisfy both pedagogic needs and aesthetic ideals as exemplified by the earlier 'iconic schools' considered in Chapter 1 (see Saint, 1987 and Maclure, 1985 for much more detail about this fascinating period of school design). As discussed in that chapter, however, it can be argued that this period of collaboration went off track through not casting the net for participants wide enough. The tendency to concentrate on the educational understanding of advisors and headteachers, rather than the experience of ordinary teachers and other staff, or the perspectives of students and parents, ended up narrowing the designers' appreciation of the school learning environment. This resulted in buildings that were fitted to certain pedagogical intentions, showing the power of educationalists' participation in school design, but these intentions did not include the wider experience of schooling at the time or over subsequent decades.

This interpretation is supported by research in the UK and elsewhere which demonstrates the range of perspectives and opinions to be found across any school community. The opinions of teachers (Schapiro, 2001; Cooper, 1985), children (Burke & Grosvenor,

2003; Cohen & Trostle, 1990) and school principals (Tanner and Langford, 2002) have been individually addressed. Although there are commonalities in these opinions (Maxwell, 2000; Douglas & Gifford, 2001), there are also differences. Some work has suggested that the main concerns of the various users of a school may differ (Fraser, 1984; Maxwell, 2000; Ornstein, 1997). So an environment that appears satisfactory to one group of users may be disappointing to another group. Even where users' values and concerns coincide, their evaluations of these aspects may differ. For example, an investigation of opinions in an American elementary school found that the parents, teachers and students all valued the display of student work, but while the adults thought that the school achieved this aim, the students were less satisfied (Maxwell, 2000).

If designers and architects can come to appreciate this range of views this would seem to increase the chances of satisfying more needs, particularly where the users' views do not directly conflict but there is disagreement about degree or extent. Of course there is a danger that such attention to the perceptions of a school community only familiar with their current situation might lead to diluting of ideals and a failure to understand potential for change. This problem will be returned to but it is worth noting that although some architects working in education find teachers conservative, Jamieson and colleagues argue that conservatism in the design of educational facilities is generally due to failing to involve users (Jamieson *et al.*, 2000). Coming from an environmental psychology background, Rivlin and Wolfe are especially positive about the ideas and vision of children, regarding their involvement in design projects as vital in overcoming the conservatism of adults (Rivlin & Wolfe, 1985). Further discussion of the conservatism, or otherwise, of particular participants will be left until the next chapter where we will look at the actual practice of collaborative design. The particular valuing of the child's perspective, which is evident in recent contributions to the school design literature (e.g. Flutter, 2006; Burke & Grosvenor, 2003), is clearly linked to the student voice movement. A more detailed discussion of these issues will follow in the section on theories of participation. It still seems reasonable to conclude, however, that when designers and architects become familiar with the range of views held across a particular school community and beyond, it is more likely that the resulting environment will be fit for all the purposes anticipated or desired.

Benefits for the participants

As the current wave of school building work on the UK got going, there were a number of initiatives which aimed to use collaborative design to raise awareness and understanding of design and the built environment. The Construction Industry Council and CABE developed the Design Quality Indicator (DQI), a method of assessing school buildings which can be used by students and staff to gain insight into their current premises and launch the designing of a new building. Although the focus with the

DQI is the building, CABE are quite clear that its use is intended to help students to develop the ability to see their school from an architectural perspective, and some of the vocabulary used reflects this intention. The underlying idea, that users are generally empowered by understanding and perhaps altering their physical setting is a popular one among architects and environmental psychologists (see e.g. David, 1975; Horne Martin, 2002).

Aimed very explicitly at directly affecting the participants, the Sorrel Foundation's Joined up design for Schools initiative (Sorrell, 2005) did not necessarily result in any physical change to the school premises. The projects concentrated on the process of finding a solution to a problem with the school environment, which the students identified, through a small group of students working as 'clients' to an established designer or architect. This allowed them to develop a range of knowledge and skills, both specific to design and, more generally, in areas such as presentation and communication. The Design Council's Schools Renaissance project included making limited changes to the school environment, but again the initiative valued the personal development of the students involved.

The School Works initiative had wider intentions, centred on redesigning a school environment for the future benefit and use of the wider school community. Their publications (e.g. Comely *et al*, 2005; Seymour *et al.*, 2001) advise on collaborations which include people from across the school. Yet in discussion of the project, it is often the personal benefits for students in terms of increased skills, cooperation and self confidence which are emphasised (Wright, 2004).

It can be seen that this impact on participants is a distinct aspect of a collaborative design and one that has been noted across projects. As well as the self evaluations mentioned above, a recent independent survey of participatory design, funded by a UK Research Council (Engineering and Physical Research Council, under title Involving Users in the School Design Process: Oct 2006–April 2010), concluded that this aspect is important:

> The process could provide new experiences within the school, giving different children the opportunity to shine and show skills which may not have been evident before. One designer/facilitator found that teachers and children were influenced by work that had been carried out by the artists in their school.... Another facilitator had experience of participating students wanting to become architects as a result of their involvement.... Also noted was the opportunity for expression of pupil voice and increased motivation that involvement in such projects can bring.
>
> Parnell *et al.*, (2008: 214–215)

To a certain extent these student experiences mirror those achieved by the numerous architectural outreach and education projects, which go on in a fairly uncelebrated way whether or not new schools are being built (Dudek, 2005; Koralek & Mitchell, 2005). For the relatively small groups of children and young people involved in these projects it appears that the impact is quite pronounced, offering them opportunities to think and work in different ways, which emphasise physical, spatial and visual, rather than verbal, understanding, as well as often developing team working and cooperative skills. There have also been initiatives intending to provide such opportunities more widely. During the 1970s in England, the Schools Council's Art and the Built Environment project flourished briefly (1976–82). This worked through schools, adding explicitly architectural elements to the secondary art curriculum (Adams & Ward 1982).

Those whose own background is in architecture are often very enthusiastic about these sorts of projects, taking the long view that developing knowledge and changing attitudes among even a few children will eventually pay dividends in the form of a more 'visually literate' population. Such conclusions are also appealing to educators who are not developing children's reading or cookery skills, for instance, only with immediate improvement in mind, but also to support them to become adults who can read widely and feed themselves well. Recent focus on 'life-long learning' may have made this idea more explicit, but it is clearly pre-existing and is evident in aspects of the curriculum and the attitudes of teaching staff.

Yet, valid as these design and architecture based enrichment activities might be in general educational terms, in the meantime a school building project might be occurring, which shifts the focus from the development of participants to the development of the actual physical environment. As we have seen above, it is clearly possible for the involvement of users to affect the design process and there are, additionally, these impacts on the individuals themselves. How are these two aspects to be integrated and made mutually beneficial?

I would argue that the key here is to widen the range of participants to include teachers, who are often involved more peripherally, and other school staff, parents and the wider community, who are generally forgotten. Architects who work in education settings are often keen that teachers are helped to develop an understanding of the physical environment. Dudek (2000:50–55) discusses in some detail how working with teachers to develop their appreciation of their classrooms as physical settings enables them to play a much more central role in the process of designing a new school or classroom. In this he recalls previous calls for training for teachers so they can contribute to school building plans (NUT England, 1974). More recently, architect Sandra Horne-Martin has repeatedly called for 'environmental awareness' to be part of teacher training and continuing professional development (Horne-Martin, 2002; 2006), arguing that developing their appreciation of the physical environment would enable teachers to make better and more thoughtful use of the physical space they have for teaching. From this perspective, participatory design of a new or refurbished setting, as part of a school level building project such as BSF, could, if carefully conducted, provide a springboard that encourages both teachers and learners, and presumably other staff in the school, to become more thoughtful and involved users of their environment. This idea of developing both the building and its inhabitants, with an eye on longer term physical, personal and social benefits will be considered next.

Benefits for the Future

There is perhaps a tendency for both architects and educators to see the physical setting and the learning activities of the users as relatively or potentially separate. Environmental psychologists, however, seem more inclined to see these two aspects of the environment as more fundamentally interlinked. For example, they use the concept of 'affordances', which are the possibilities provided by the environment to a user with certain skills and inclinations (Clark & Uzzell, 2006; Kytta, 2006). These exist at the interface of the person and their environment, and require an understanding of the relationship between them. More concretely, Sundstrom (1987) reports findings of increased satisfaction in workplaces which were designed through user involvement with the comment that this satisfaction could be due to the involvement itself, the resulting building actually being better ... or perhaps both.

From the preceding sections, there would seem to be value in both these reasons for increased satisfaction and, particularly, in the interplay between the two as time goes on. The perspective offered by environmental psychology reminds us that the relationship of the user to the environment is not set in stone, but will, or should, respond to the shifting sands of human abilities, needs and desires. The value of such an on-going dynamic relationship, which might be set off by collaborative design, is suggested by the comments of many advocates of participation in the design process. As we have seen, Horne-Martin argues that teachers' abilities to make good use of their space will increase through their engaging with design and architecture. She anticipates that this will make teachers more confident; more inclined and able to reorganise their classrooms according to their pedagogical intentions, and avoid them being 'reduced to defensive postures' in their use of space (2006: 101).

This understanding of an environment is particularly important when it has been substantially altered or rebuilt, as is currently happening in many schools. Post occupancy surveys often reveal problems with buildings which are partly due to users not really knowing how to use them (e.g. DfES, 2006), while architects can be very critical of teachers using schools 'wrongly'. Participation in the design process, so that users appreciate general ideas about the use of space and also understand the particular case of their new school should be extremely valuable.

It seems likely that any impact of participatory design on teachers will also be seen in the content and style of their teaching, not just in how they arrange their room or cope with a new building. Facilitators of participatory design surveyed by Parnell *et al.* (2008) mentioned such potential impact on the curriculum, both while the projects are occurring and,hopefully, afterwards:

> Many different learning opportunities were noted for the students and their teachers, perhaps the most direct being the development of 'spatial skills', . . . the value of using real life experiences as learning experiences, the opportunity to link different aspects of the curriculum.
>
> Parnell et al., (2008: 215)

It is hoped, therefore, by those involved that the impact of participatory design goes beyond altering the attitudes or behaviour of some individuals to affect the culture of the school in the longer term. This suggests how a school community might be able to continue to appreciate its new building once the immediate 'wow' factor has dulled a little and the students who were personally involved at the design stage have moved on.

It might appear, however, that this is beginning to imply a one-way learning process, where participation in design affects the school building itself and the intertwined practice of its inhabitants, but has no impact on the architects and designers. Since this book is primarily aimed at educators, rather than architects, the detail of such learning does not concern us but it does seem important to note the need for designers and architects to continue to develop their understanding of education. Participatory design has the potential to ensure that they do. As architect, Jeremy Till points out, 'true participation demands that the process is two-way – that the user should have the opportunity to actively transform the knowledge of the architect' (Till, 2005: 33). It might be argued that the assumptions made in the 1970s by school architects about educational practices would have been more nuanced if they had had more direct contact with teachers, students and parents. Certainly the rather formulaic design of primary schools according to half-understood open-planning principles, and the rolling out of standard designs which occurred at this time (Woolner *et al.*, 2005; Bennett *et al.*, 1980) do not suggest developing architectural ideas or learning from particular school settings.

This is not to blame individuals, of course, since for continued collaboration and participation opportunities need to be available for the architects as they do for the educators. How this might be facilitated is a further consideration for the next chapter when the practice of participation will be investigated. To summarise here, we have seen how the potential benefits of participatory design encompass influencing the altered environment itself, for good or ill, and the participants, over the short and, perhaps, the longer term. Importantly, it seems that the potential for longer term influence is bound up with recognising and understanding the inextricable linking of actor and setting. Encouraging the development of a dynamic understanding should allow for some continual updating of knowledge and practice on the part of both educators and architects. If this can occur, participatory design suggests a way to satisfy the needs of architects and educationalists (e.g. Dudek, 2000 and Clark, 2002, respectively) who have called for more involvement of users in school design and a better understanding of the practical contribution of the physical setting to teaching and learning.

Types of collaboration and participation

The foregoing discussion of the wide-ranging potential benefits of participation in design is very positive and uplifting but begs the question of why, if it's such a good idea, participation in practice can often be so disappointing. This is the issue which architect Jeremy Till, considering the theory and practice of participation in planning and architecture, spotlights graphically by describing a thinly attended public meeting where the local government officer does 'a remarkable job in motivating some response out of the slumped bodies, the dropped shoulders, out of people numbed by years of failed promises' (Till, 2005:23). Although a 'cursory discussion' has taken place and a vote occurs, this meeting does not seem to be indicative of the genuine participation claimed by such events.

In the context of designing for education, researchers who investigated the 1960s-70s wave of school building expressed doubts that the consultation of teachers was really valued. Bennett and colleagues suggested that, 'Even when consultation is offered, there is evidence that motives are often political rather than a genuine desire to assure constructive involvement' (Bennett *et al.*, 1980: 89). The NUT report of the time (NUT (England) 1974) makes related points about pseudo-consultation and the lack of involvement of teachers (p. 6, paragraph 24). A teacher in further education I spoke to informally had experienced a consultation process some years ago which had made him very cynical. Angrily he pointed to a canteen dining table, saying that if that was imagined as the size of the planned college discussed with teachers then the size of the finished building was no bigger than a saucer!

Terms used in this context are clearly important. Consultation, however thorough, suggests a one-way flow of information, from the users to the designers. This, in turn, implies a rather passive role for the users as suppliers of the information which is deemed important by the designers, perhaps not including the information or aspects of their experience that the users consider to be important. Attaching more active labels, such as participation or involvement, to a process, however, will not guarantee that these activities are taken to enough depth or valued sufficiently by the participants to provide the benefits of genuine collaboration. Getting to grips with what constitutes a poor or better participatory process should help all those involved in one to make the most of opportunities offered, know where it might be appropriate to demand more and avoid simply becoming cynical about the whole idea. So how are we to judge the quality of a participatory process?

Ladders and levels

In this endeavour, we are helped by some discussions which occurred in the context of planning in the 1960s. As mentioned previously, practitioners and theorists of planning have been grappling with these issues for some time and, in 1969, Shelley Arnstein published a seminal article proposing a 'ladder of citizen participation'. This used a typology to describe how people might be involved in the planning and operation of public programmes. This views participation as ranging from 'manipulation', where ideas are basically imposed on users, through 'informing' and 'consultation', which can be of limited worth if done in isolation, to the genuine participation of 'partnership' and 'citizen control' (Arnstein, 1969). Roger Hart adapted this idea of a ladder to describe how children and young people might be involved in projects of all sorts, with their participation ranging through tokenistic inclusion to genuine partnership with adults (see e.g. Hart, 1987; 1997). Hart has applied this conception specifically to children's involvement in architecture and design, as well as to other projects.

Equally relevant to the issue of participatory school design is educationalist Michael Fielding's categorisation of four levels of student involvement in educational research (Fielding, 2001b). His student voice typology goes from students as data source, through their being active respondents up to students as co-researchers and, finally, researchers. At the most basic level, equating to consultation in the context of planning and designing a new school setting, students are seen as passive sources of information. As the typologies of Arnstein and Hart remind us, this level of involvement in the design process can be carried out more or less honestly: sometimes genuinely seeking information, but sometimes trying to manipulate or offer token involvement. At the higher levels in all the typologies, there is what might be termed genuine participation, where organisers and participants both have real inputs and it seems possible that a shared understanding might result. The three typologies all have a top level where the 'participant' of the previous levels is actually in control of the process . In the context of school building, with a project ultimately controlled by external organisations, such as central government in the case of BSF, it seems unrealistic to expect this sort of level of participation to be achieved. It seems reasonable, however, that a participatory design process should aspire to be genuinely collaborative with the users in school and the designers outside, neither of whom are completely in control, working in partnership.

Adding more dimensions to ladders of participation

These conceptions of ladders of participation are extremely useful in conveying the sense that any act of participation has a level or extent, and they can clearly assist any attempt to assess or evaluate an example of participation. Through discovering aspects of a would-be participatory exercise that reveal its intention to inform, or worse, manipulate participants, thereby placing the exercise low on a ladder of participation, it is possible to critique the exercise and suggest improvements that could move it up the ladder. An example of this use of the conception is provided by an adaptation of Arnstein's ladder to the context of designing school grounds (Sheat & Beer, 1994: 94).

As soon as we try to apply these conceptions of levels closely to the context of whole school communities participating in the complex and long process of a school rebuild, however, two major limitations become obvious. These concern the process not being a single event and the different groups that comprise the school community. To deal firstly with the length of the process, it is not clear whether we should see the whole process as requiring one rating for the extent of its participation, or whether the various stages – initial 'visioning', more detailed planning, building, opening the building for use and finally any post-occupancy evaluation or trouble-shooting – should each be rated. It would presumably depend on individual circumstances and the function of any assessment.

More fundamental is the problem that all three typologies of participation are designed to categorise the involvement of single particular groups of people, either citizens, children and young people or pupils and students. Although all these groupings are wide it is possible, in the appropriate context, to talk sensibly about them as single groups. In the context of understanding and improving the design of a school, however, there are a number of quite distinct groups of people. The school community might be seen as comprising senior managers, classroom teachers, teaching supporters, non-teaching staff, students, parents, governors and the wider community. Educationalists have written about the hierarchies inherent in school structure and often focus on the power disparities between adults and children, particularly in discussions of student voice. For example, Catherine Burke reminds us that, 'schools are places where adults are in positions of power over children' (2007: 363). Yet it is clear that in such a hierarchical organisation as a school, power disparities also exist between adult groups. This has been pointed out by innovators and trainers who work in schools with non-teaching staff. For example a group of educationalists who both research and professionally develop teaching assistants (TAS) comment that these people have been 'perceived to be at the bottom of the staff hierarchy' (Dunne *et al.*, 2008). Further, in a tellingly titled chapter, 'You're only a dinner lady!', Gil Fell describes how lunchtime supervisors were pleased, though surprised, to be involved in improvements to breaktimes since their jobs have low status and they do not feel respected by students or teachers (Fell, 1994).

Therefore in the context of participatory school design, we need to inquire who is participating, as well as questioning what level that participation amounts to. Through the examination of the previous sections of the benefits for the school building and its occupants it became clear that wider participation should reap more benefits. Taken together this suggests the validity of a participatory design process will depend on who is involved and where their involvement rates on a ladder of participation. It might be helpful to see this as adding another dimension to the ladder (see Figure 4.1 below).

Returning to the discussion of stages of the process, the different stages in the design, building and use of the new learning environment could be subsumed by the levels of participation dimension, if it is argued that genuine partnership requires, by definition, participation through all the design stages. Alternatively, the stages of the process could be seen as adding a third dimension to the typologies above.

Levels of Participation	partnership							
	collaboration							
	involvement							
	consultation							
		senior management	teachers	learning support	other staff	students	parents	others
		People involved						

Figure 4.1 A two dimensional ladder of participation in school design

The central purpose of the participation

It might be questioned whether such a burgeoning system of levels and groups is getting out of control, revealing the inevitable complications of any school design situation but without adding much to our understanding. In essence these typologies are trying to help us determine whether a participatory process is a genuine, honest attempt at collaboration or a quick fix, minimally fulfilling a statuary duty through ensuring 'boxes are ticked'. To this end it is important how the process is conducted, which is where the 'ladders' come in, and I have argued additionally for the importance of who is involved. Although the question of which groups of people are actively involved is particularly central to a school design project, the importance of who is involved in any participatory process has been noted by others studying this area. For example, Richardson and Connelly discuss in some detail how particpation in the planning process might be compromised through excluding people from the process (Richardson & Connelly, 2005: 90–94).

Once lots of different people are involved in a participatory process, however, the question of how it is conducted becomes considerably more difficult. It is not enough just to ensure an adequate level of input for each participant, or group of participants: we need further to organise the interactions of their inputs. In a school design project, what is to be done if the experiences of the various groups differ so much that their opinions and desires actually conflict?

What seems central in deciding how to deal with these difficulties, and should help us assess the validity of a process, is returning to the central purpose of the collaboration: is participation really desired and valued, or is this a box-ticking exercise? It seems to me that this question of why participation is being attempted, hard though it is to answer, includes the who and the how aspects to the endeavour. As far as resolving the dilemma of conflicting views is concerned, if the why question can be answered by a genuine, democratic commitment to developing shared understandings through participation in the design process, then a solution may lie in dialogue. This might appear trite, but it seems unavoidable that only through open discussion by equally valued groups will it be possible for people to begin to understand each other. Participants may not agree on everything, but they should, through dialogue, be able to appreciate the reasons for any disagreements and begin to decide on resolutions.

Many explorations of participation argue that communication is central to any successful participatory process. In their reflections on participation in planning decisions, Richardson & Connelly (2005) argue that these processes fail to be genuinely participatory through imposing limitations on discussion by excluding people, issues or outcomes (p.90) and producing 'bland statements which can be agreed by all' (p.98). Conclusions about dialogue are also reached by Jeremy Till, whose description of unsatisfactory participation in architecture opened this section. He praises the idea of 'design as making-sense-together' (Till, 2005: 39) and argues that '[t]he key lies in recognising the power and validity of ordinary conversation as a starting point for the participatory process' (*ibid*: 37).

This reasoning has parallels within recent theorising about student voice, which has argued for the 'building of a shared dialogue' (Lodge, 2005: 134) and the importance of questioning 'who is listening?' to student voices (Fielding, 2001a: 102). Also, paralleling some critiques of the student voice movement (Moore & Muller, 1999), it is important not to perceive the experiences and views of school users regarding their environment as static, 'authentic' truths, which cannot be discussed or changed, since in some ways this renders the experiences or voices more purely individual and easier to ignore. Although there are undoubtedly problems of power and influence in a school, people's views must be open to question or the myriad of varying views and opinions risk all being brushed under the carpet as equally valid, but equally ignorable. Without a collaborative attempt being made to consider and resolve conflicting views, there is the danger of many individual acts of participation amounting to very little, in much the same way as some researchers fear that student voice may come to involve lots of shouting without much attempt at interpretation or understanding.

Conclusion

In this chapter, it has been argued that a collaborative design process is key to understanding, and hopefully responding to, the disparate, often contrasting, sometimes conflicting, views and experiences of school community members. Given that an ideal physical learning environment does not seem definable, attempting to fit new or refurbished school premises to the needs and desires of the potential users seems a valid approach. In addition, we have seen that there is considerable evidence of benefits resulting from participatory processes, where these involve architecture or design, which can be related to similar advantages claimed for participation in other processes within education, or indeed for the more general ideal of participation.

These benefits are generally agreed to include positive impacts on those involved, which many writers consider to be reason enough for participation. In the foregoing discussion, however, the assumed benefits to the individual participants were linked to the desired outcomes for the physical environment. It was argued that the learning environment offered by the school premises can only be fully understood if the relationship of the building to its users is considered carefully, and preferably developed, through a participatory process of redesign. The design process should then benefit the users involved, the building they help to design and the future use of the building, with this usage understood as a dynamic, ongoing relationship between people and setting.

It seems clear that to achieve such results it is necessary to involve a wide range of users of the school. Otherwise this positive dynamic could be limited to only a subset of the school community, and perhaps be lost as they move on. Such an inclusive approach to participation is argued to be beneficial both within the context of design projects and beyond, but is clearly not simple to achieve. More participants, especially if they are drawn from quite disparate groups across the school inevitably make successful participatory events more challenging. As we have seen, there is anyway potential for so-called participation to amount to no more than informing people of previously made decisions, or even manipulating them to believe that they have contributed. This tendency for some participation to be mere window-dressing has been discussed and criticised by planners, architects and others over the last forty years, yet would still seem to be a problem. Widening the range of participants perhaps makes such limited involvement more likely, at least for some groups of participants. Recent critiques of the student or pupil 'voice' movement in education should raise awareness of the challenges inherent in not just letting people speak but also listening to them, facilitating their interaction with each other and learning from their experiences. If participatory design processes are not conducted carefully and with integrity, the participation achieved could be more like the 'parallel play' seen in toddlers than the genuine dialogue required to produce the shared understanding and actual collaboration necessary to design a suitable new learning environment.

5 Collaborative School Design: making it work

Introduction

In the previous chapter I examined why the process to design a new learning environment should be participatory. There is an expectation, and often an official requirement, that school users will be involved in any rebuilding or refurbishment. So the opportunity exists and, I have argued, potential benefits of participation in the design process can be identified for the building, the inhabitants and the way that the environment is understood and used as time goes on. Furthermore, the recent history of school construction in the UK suggests the benefit of community engagement and shared purpose, as against the problems of architects failing to understand the experience of actual school communities. This does not mean, however, that any participation, however conceived, will be sufficient. In the last chapter, I considered various ways of assessing the quality of participatory processes and found that the level of participation is generally judged to be central, but that considering who is involved is also important. This seems especially vital in the context of a school community, where there are distinct groups of people, with very different relationships to the school, and a complex web of power relations. Once a wide range of people are involved in a participatory process, however, this potentially produces problems of very different, or actually conflicting, views. Difficult though this might be to manage, never mind resolve, I have argued that the solution must lie in dialogue and, therefore, the closer a participatory process can get to being genuinely collaborative, the more valid it is, and the more likely it is to succeed in the terms discussed earlier.

We now turn to discovering how these theoretical aims might be realised in practice. Although it has been argued that full collaboration should be seen as the ideal form of participatory school design, this is not to dismiss less developed participatory processes and, in this chapter, we will be examining attempts as various levels and considering their implications for participatory design in general. In doing this, it is worth remembering that even a fairly basic level of participation can be much appreciated by participants, and may still have the power to produce interesting insights, perhaps even contributing to the school community becoming more open and democratic. For a flavour of this, consider the architectural facilitators interviewed by Parnell and colleagues (Parnell *et al.*, 2008). Although they focus mainly on students, their comments would seem to apply more widely:

> Students were noted as having in-depth knowledge of their school, the building and what works for them. It was recognised that through listening to them, architects, facilitators and contractors could gain an insight into how the school works. The principle of engagement was described as being effective precisely 'because nobody's ever asked them'. This was true not only of students: 'Every time we do a project with students and teachers, teachers especially say, "Nobody ever asked us".' It was felt by some that the act of asking teachers and students for their views was more important than the specific engagement technique used.
>
> Parnell *et al.*, (2008: 215)

Having reported these ideas, and other suggestions about the specific benefits to being involved in a school design project, the researchers comment that it seems 'likely that the sense of having a voice, no matter what the sphere, would have similar positive impacts on the life and culture of the school' (*ibid*: 216).

The nature of the evidence

In trying to establish ways to carry out participatory design I will be drawing on examples and ideas with various origins. Most of this is not research specifically into participatory design and, as discussed previously, even the research into learning environments in general is quite patchy. It is often possible, however, to find suggestions about the use, or absence, of participation in more general articles and books concerned with the educational setting. Therefore, I will be referring where appropriate to this, often older and sometimes more general, indicative work, as well as to more recent research centred on the relationship of the school community to its environment.

In addition, I will be drawing on the experience of our research centre (the Research Centre for Learning and Teaching, Newcastle University), which includes evaluating or other involvement with a range of school-based projects and initiatives, some quite participatory, others externally imposed. In particular, I will be referring to three projects which provided us with direct experience of participatory design in a school context. These are our evaluation of the Design Council's Schools Renaissance project (Hall & Wall, 2006; Woolner *et al.*, 2007b), our evaluation of an Arts Council project to put artists into schools and LAs as they prepared for BSF (Woolner & Hall, 2006), and our own participatory design initiative, commissioned by Durham LA (Woolner *et al.*, 2008; 2010).

In the first of these projects we were independent, external observers, able to assess the effects of participatory design conducted by design professionals with teachers and students in three secondary schools. We evaluated the process from initiation through to the completion and use of some changes to the environment, with a particular interest in the views and understandings of the process developed by the school participants. The second project was less clearly participatory but provided valuable insights into the tensions inherent in situations where schools and educators try to accommodate artistic and architectural ideas and people. The third project involved conducting an initial consultation for a school expecting to be included in BSF, and we used the opportunity to explore the use of a range of participatory visually-based research tools with participants who included students (aged 11 to 16), teachers (with various levels of experience and responsibility), learning support staff, technicians and other non-teaching staff, including office staff, lunchtime supervisors and cleaners.

Finally, in addition to this formal knowledge, both direct and indirect, I am influenced by the on-going experience of visiting schools, observing how they are used and talking to heads, teachers and learners about learning and the places where it happens. Increasingly, as more schools are refurbished or rebuilt, this less formal contact includes meeting people with recent, or current, experience of their school environment being radically changed. Although these informal experiences risk a descent into anecdote, I think they form a vital part of our growing understanding of school design. As BSF began, concerns were expressed by architects and those in the construction industry that the long lull in school building in the UK had resulted in a worrying dearth of experience in school design, procurement and construction (Spring, 2004). As that begins to change, and experience is developing in both the educational and architectural worlds about the process of designing new educational spaces, it seems important that books such as this one attempt to convey some of this growing knowledge.

Chapter organisation

As has been discussed, participation can happen at any stage of the design process. It seems important that it is not seen as an isolated instance, and a more iterative approach seems more likely to be effective. Currently, though, Parnell reports that 'efforts tend to be disorganised or stand-alone, rarely dove-tailed into ongoing work by the design and construction team. This can lead to disappointment and frustration, not only for schools, but also for designers' (Parnell *et al.*, 2008: 222). Thus it does not seem possible at this time to discuss ideas for each stage of the design process or consider exactly how these might be knitted together (for some ideas on participatory techniques for particular stages in the design of school grounds, see Sheat & Beer, 1994; for ideas linked to stages in the process of school design, see the School Works Toolkit, Seymour *et al*, 2001). Therefore this chapter will not be organised through the stages of the process but will make suggestions which should be seen as applying to any, and, perhaps, every stage of the process.

In fact the organisation that has been chosen for this chapter might appear to contradict one of the central ideas so far developed: that of very wide participation. It might seem that this central idea is undermined by the decision to consider participation of particular groups of people, which could be interpreted as suggesting that some groups can be left out. This is not the intention, however, and I hope that enough evidence and argument has been developed in the foregoing chapters to make that case convincingly. It must be admitted, however, that despite the rationale for general participation, there are particular issues involved in the participation of particular groups from the school community and particular qualities that they will tend to bring to the process (see table 1). There is, furthermore, a lot more evidence and experience on which to draw in the case of some groups than there is for others.

Participant group	Issues	Qualities
Students	representative samples age experience power appropriate methods	wide-ranging, detailed knowledge and experience more imaginative?
Teachers	conservatism many other demands clash of professional cultures continued involvement	link to curriculum detailed knowledge and experience day to day control of classrooms link to school's past link to school's future
Parents	representative samples dated ideas about education limited knowledge of current school experience	critical distance but very interested
Other school staff	power and status confidence continued involvement pay, time to be involved appropriate methods	detailed knowledge and experience unusual viewpoints overview of school organisation community viewpoint link to school's past link to school's future
Wider community	representative samples limited, dated knowledge specific, limited concerns	community viewpoint link to school's past

Figure 5.1 Qualities and issues associated with participant groups from a school community

Participation of the school community in the design process

Students

Although school students were rarely, if ever, directly included in the design and construction of previous waves of British schools, they are now the group who are most commonly suggested for inclusion in consultations and participatory events. Many of the organisations and initiatives recently established as part of the new wave of school construction have particularly targeted school students, usually on the basis that they know their school, and the activities which take place there, particularly intimately. So, for example, describing the School Works initiative, Sharon Wright comments that 'it was the pupils who gave us some of the most useful insights into what needed to be different. We simply cannot believe that school design will be effective without asking pupils their views' (Wright, 2004: 42).

This targeting means that there are numerous quite recent research reports, pamphlets and other publications suggesting how students might be enabled to participate in a design process, and proposing some of the benefits of helping them to do so. As discussed previously, such targeting of students in the context of school design should be seen as a part of a much more general trend to allow children and young people a 'voice'. As a result, some of the research reporting initial attempts to involve students in discussing or planning school environments has been produced by researchers within a student voice framework who see school design as another area where students should be involved (Könings *et al.*, 2007; Flutter, 2006; Frost & Holden, 2008). Interestingly, researchers from this perspective can see student involvement in decisions about the school environment as a relatively safe way for students to participate in school planning or organisation: 'Issues about the environment are also a relatively comfortable topic for teachers to explore with students whereas inviting students to comment on teaching can be difficult for both teachers and students where consultation is new' (Flutter, 2006: 191).

Both in the context of school design, and within the student voice movement more generally, there is a need to ensure that there is substance to the initiatives, and not just appealing-sounding rhetoric. This involves considering who within the student body is being given the opportunity to participate and examining the purpose of their participation. There are plenty of warnings about isolated, tokenistic initiatives which can leave students feeling frustrated and cynical (e.g. Parnell *et al.*, 2008; Matthews & Limb, 2003; Sheat & Beer, 1994). A review of initiatives involving young people in public decision-making conducted in 2002 concluded there is certainly distrust and cynicism among young people who do not get involved in such participation, and that this might sometimes be caused by previous tokenistic involvement (Kirby, 2002).

Moving on from the direct benefits for the students, and the anticipated increases in openness and democracy, which those working within a student voice framework tend to emphasise, there are often clear benefits for the future of the learning environment in including students in its design. Or, more precisely, there are numerous reports of the problems of failing to include students. In their book about children's relationships with institutional settings, including schools, Rivlin and Wolfe describe an occasion where not involving pupils in an exciting classroom innovation fatally undermined it ('the loft structure that "suddenly appeared"', 1985: 200) and Flutter points out that 'when students are not consulted about proposed changes to their environment, their response to 'improvements' can sometimes be oppositional' (2006: 186). In a classic article about curriculum innovation, Jean Rudduck remarks that 'pupils' definitions of school and classroom behaviour can be powerful conservative forces in educational practice' (1980: 142). Through my involvement with practitioner research, I have more recently encountered examples of teaching and learning innovations, usually decided upon by the teacher and perhaps not adequately negotiated with the learners, which students have disliked, criticised or failed to co-operate with.

Issues to consider when involving students

A key issue is that of representation. It might be possible to involve all the students in some initial surveying or 'design day' event. It is likely, however, that at some stage, if the student input is to be continued and form a real part of the process, there will need to be some sampling from the student body and it is important how this is done. To benefit the consultative aspect of the students' involvement, it will make sense to have a range of ages and interests represented. Furthermore, in considering the consultative aspect of student involvement, it might be easier and seemingly more productive to target more forthcoming, confident or keen students. Here the student voice perspective is useful in reminding us of the pitfalls with such an approach:

> Some voices (e.g. middle class girls) seem to be more willing to speak than others, partly because they may feel more at ease with the way teachers speak about students and with the capacity of schools to understand what matters in their daily lives. This more differentiated awareness of student voice thus raises issues of validity and the degree to which some students can legitimately speak on behalf of others.
>
> Fielding, (2001a: 101)

To reduce bias due to adult preferences, a possibility is for students to elect representatives. Recent experience of youth councils working within local authorities, however, demonstrate that having elections does not result in councils which are representative of their constituencies in terms of age, gender or ethnicity. Also, those involved, and those left out, rapidly start to make assumptions about the sort of people who sit on youth councils, making it progressively harder to increase inclusivity (Matthew & Limb, 2003).

Clearly there is no easy answer to completely solve the problem of sampling students. It might help to form student groups focusing on particular aspects of the redesigned environment, so producing a rationale for including students with divergent interests. This could allow groupings around, for example, library facilities, catering, sport, etc., but it will presumably be much more awkward to recruit appropriate students for groups working on anti-social behaviour, exclusions, or student apathy, despite a need to get an insider view on these parts of school experience. Suggestive of the possible difficulties of this sort of approach is the experience of a participatory research project that attempted to deploy disadvantaged young people to interview their peers. Many problems ensued, such as would-be student researchers failing to come to training sessions, and in the end the project recruited a social science undergraduate who seemed successful in relating to young people to conduct the interviews (Robson, 2001).

Whatever the method of recruiting students to participate in a school design project, a key consideration when involving children is their age. There is the need to ensure that the activities are approximately appropriate in terms of demands on reading or writing skills, levels of concentration and style of presentation, for example. There are, however, many suggestions for techniques and activities that can be used with even very young children as part of a participatory design process. The more purely architectural and design-based approaches tend to require visual, spatial or practical skills, rather than making demands on literacy (see, e.g. Dudek, 2005). These are often more about appreciating shape and space in general, however, rather than developing particular ideas about requirement for a new learning space, and will, in addition, often require practical skills, such as accurate cutting or measuring, which could be beyond very young children.

The 'Mosaic' approach (Clark, 2005) has been developed specifically to enable such young children to become engaged in discussions about their surroundings. Clark argues that the range of activities with the children is necessary to capture the 'complexity of their everyday lives' (2005: 10). Furthermore, the visual and physical basis of the methods focus on 'young children's strengths – their local knowledge, their attention to detail, and their visual as well as verbal communication skills' (p.10). Thus the approach makes use of photographs and drawings produced by the children, guided walks round the environment and lots of spoken discussion. By using a variety of methods, the approach intends that more children can get involved and more aspects of the environment are brought to light.

Other tool kits for inclusive approaches to school design similarly suggest using a variety of, hopefully, interesting activities (Harnell-Young & Fisher, 2007; Wright, 2004). I have written elsewhere about the benefits of using a range of introductory activities, some based on maps or plans, and some on photographs, to help participants of all ages start to think about their learning environment (Woolner *et al.*, 2008; 2010).

Of course there are also general methods for engaging with children described within the wider educational literature, which might be adapted to the needs of a participatory design project. This includes teaching and learning techniques which can be found in the professional literature, and with which teachers are often familiar, that can be adapted. For example, we have made use of 'diamond ranking', a thinking skills technique (Rockett & Percival 2002: 99) to support the ranking of pictures of school features and places (Woolner *et al.*, 2008; 2010). Figure 5.2 below shows two Year 7 students engaging with a diamond ranking activity (left) and the annotated ranking produced by Year 8 students as part of our initial consultation in their school.

Asking primary school age children to draw their classroom has been found to reveal ideas about learning (Lodge, 2007), and could be used as an introduction to a redesign project. A more structured approach to asking about learning in particular situations is possible using 'pupil view templates', which require children to fill in speech and thought bubbles for figures taking part in familiar school activities (Wall, 2008). Through scribing for children if necessary, these can be used with quite young children and can be very revealing of what children think about an activity or place. Another way to add structure, and perhaps avoid being over demanding on drawing skills, is through the use of collage. Asking adolescents to put together 'scrapbooks' has been found to be a successful way for them to communicate ideas, especially if they feel shy (Bragg & Buckingham, 2008). Although the content of the project that reported this method was not school design, the activity could clearly be adapted. As an indication of this, a special school for autistic children that was involved in a project we evaluated had used collage as a less verbally demanding way for their pupils to communicate their preferences for the anticipated new school premises.

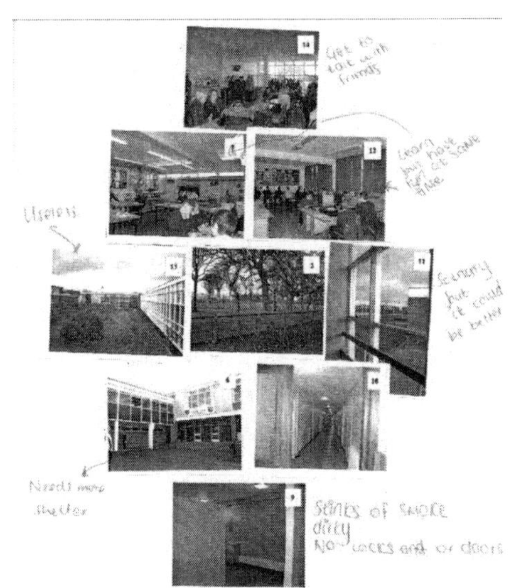

Figure 5.2 Diamond ranking activity to reveal experiences of the school

It can be seen then that there is a wealth of established methods for engaging with students of various ages and inclinations, which could also be used with other participants in a school design project. For a participatory process in a particular school, the question of absolute age is complicated by considerations of students' relative age within the school. Although the older children in the school might be more technically capable, with better literacy skills and perhaps more confidence, as well as having more experience of the school, they are also the ones who will soon be moving on and so unable to see the process through to its conclusion. This conflicts with the ideal of an on-going collaboration with the continued participation of users. It is also potentially frustrating for students. At a primary school which had had its refurbishment delayed, the headteacher spoke of doing consultation work with children who were now long gone:

> At beginning we involved a lot of children. We used School Works, visited buildings ... [But now] virtually all children involved in that process have now left the school and never saw a brick laid
>
> Woolner & Hall, (2006: 33)

For this reason of older students not expecting to use the new school, it is sometimes suggested that they will be less interested in being involved with a design process. Our experience on this is mixed. While it is true that some older secondary school students we have worked with have expressed this lack of incentive, others have been very keen to share their experience and knowledge of their school for the benefit of future students. Other instances of students taking a longer view of their involvement have also been reported. Sharon Wright describes talking to a student who had participated in the School Works project at Kingsdale School: 'she told me she plans to be a teacher and would like to come back to Kingsdale [...] She is delighted that her younger brother will benefit from an innovative building' (2004: 42). This attitude seems most likely to be found if the school has a strong community base and older students can immediately imagine younger relations and neighbours who will attend the school in its new building.

Although a detailed knowledge and intimate experience of the school, the possession of which is a solid reason for involving students, might be more developed in older students, it still seems important to involve younger students. As discussed above, there are methods available to ensure the inclusion of even very young children, and students with less experience across the school may be in a better position to describe particular aspects, which the older students have since forgotten about. For instance, during the consultation we conducted in a secondary school, all the students and staff mentioned circulation problems within the existing building, but it was the younger students who really focused on them, describing vividly the crushes in stairwells, doorways and on particular corridors.

Aside from this detailed knowledge of the day to day school experience, the other reason often given for involving school students in a design project is their ability to be more imaginative and less conservative than adults. This has certainly been a common impression of professionals from outside education when they have worked with children on projects concerning their physical environment (Dudek, 2005; Rivlin & Wolfe, 1985). An architect, talking about her recent involvement with school design projects in the UK 'found the process of working with children to be not only informative, but inspiring, as the designs 'poured out of her' based on the children's input' (Parnell *et al.*, 2008: 215). Although such inspiration might seem indicative, it should be questioned whether the input from children is actually qualitatively different from that of other user-participants. In this connection, it is worth remembering the stories of students opposing or undermining innovation. Even if these instances can be explained by inadequate communication or lack of proper involvement, they do serve to question the bland assumption that children and young people are always forward thinking and imaginative, never reactionary or conservative.

A distinct problem we have experienced in connection with the imaginative ideas of young participants is that they generally do not have much power, or the accompanying responsibility. As we have described elsewhere in more detail, this can mean that even quite vague ideas are seized by architects or designers and developed into elaborate conceptions, without reference back to the originator of the idea, but with the justification perhaps that the result is what the user wanted. At a school involved in the Schools Renaissance project, we watched as this occurred:

> Initially the school were interested in developing effective storage for the newly refurbished Geography Department [...] However, during the immersion days, where students worked alongside teachers and the Design Council team, one student produced a drawing of a classroom which looked like an amphitheatre and the designers picked on this idea and developed it [...] At some point after this, the focus moved away from storage and became about producing a 'classroom of the future' with the emphasis on flexibility of movement through 360°.
>
> Woolner *et al.*, (2007b)

Although this could happen to any idea produced by a participant, it may be that the ideas of children and young people are particularly prone to this problem due to the mismatch between their lack of power in the adult world but the high status given by that adult world to their imaginations and ideas.

This issue of power also has implications for the organisation of the participatory process. The ideals of dialogue and communication might suggest that any groups working together during a project should include mixtures of participants: students, teachers and other staff all working together. Furthermore, architects and enablers are enthusiastic about the potential of a shared design process to help teachers 'see children in a new light' (Parnell *et al.*, 2008:126). Yet it might in fact compromise these ambitions, particularly at the beginning of a process, if students are obliged to work on a supposedly equal basis with teachers with whom they usually have a quite different relationship. It can also put teachers in a difficult position if the detail of their role is not made clear and they are unsure whether they are expected to maintain, or override, their usual responsibility for supervision and order. The first of these concerns, about power relations inhibiting the design process, could also be raised in relation to teachers of very different seniority working together, and we will discuss this issue further in connection with involving non-teaching staff in the design process. It seems sensible o consider this aspect carefully when initiating a participatory design process in a particular context and to recognise that, at least in the early stages, more homogenous groupings of participants might be appropriate.

Teachers

Historically, teachers were the most likely school users to be directly involved in school design. As mentioned previously, however, participating teachers tended to be in senior or advisory roles, and the more forward looking or 'progressive' individuals were sought out (Woolner *et al.*, 2005; Cooper, 1981). The current wave of school building is supportive of more general user involvement and, in schools, some teachers have become very involved in the management of rebuilding work. This often does not extend beyond the headteacher, however, with, in a secondary school, whichever of the assistant heads has taken responsibility for managing the school's side of the process. Both anecdotal evidence and recent quantitative surveying by the evaluators of BSF (PricewaterhouseCoopers, 2007; 2008) show that, in practice, it is still the case that not many classroom teachers are participating in the redesign of their schools.

Having pointed this out, commenting that teachers are often surprised if they are asked to be involved, Parnell and colleagues discuss why, from the perspective of architects, they feel that teacher participation is important: 'Involving teachers in the process gives them the opportunity to create spaces to which they can contribute, understand, control and use effectively in the future. They might also be more forgiving about the things that do not work so well' (2008: 220). As discussed in Chapter 4, teachers are an important potential link with the future of the school through their development of the curriculum together with their continuing use of the space. The historic example of the development of open-plan classrooms in primary schools, which many teachers saw as an imposition, demonstrates potential for teachers who do not understand, or do not accept, an innovation to work against the intentions of the design. Teachers who did not want, or did not know how, to work in the way suggested by the new more open environment often attempted to ignore their surroundings, producing an awkward mismatch between the setting and their practice (Gump, 1975; Rivlin & Rothenberg, 1976; McMillan, 1983; Bennett *et al.*, 1980).

Issues to consider when involving teachers

The architects and facilitators interviewed by Parnell and colleagues were generally enthusiastic in principle about involving teachers in school design. Yet they also complained that on some occasions 'teachers were not excited by the project and did not feel involved' (Parnell *et al.*, 2008: 220). A clue to why this might be the case is given a little later on the same page, when it is remarked that 'teachers need to be assigned a role within the process. When asked to attend participatory workshops without a specific role, they tended to loiter, interfere or disappear'. This suggests that in some participatory projects teachers are just being invited along, perhaps to help organise the students, and do not feel that their professional knowledge of the school, or education more generally, is being valued. As well as contributing to their perceived lack of excitement, this also undermines the reasons discussed above for involving teachers: the aims of making links between current practice, the teachers on-going experience and the future classroom environment. It seems necessary that the role given to teachers during a school design process is explicitly related to their knowledge of school life, and genuinely values their potential to embed the new environment within continuing and developing practice.

In the wider context of school change or reform, a study of six secondary schools in the 1980s drew the tentative conclusion that 'the direct involvement of staff seemed to have played a part in encouraging school-wide innovation' (Ouston, *et al.*, 1991). In a review of school change, Pat Thomson has argued that the genuine commitment of practising classroom teachers is vital (Thomson, 2007: 38–39), but also notes the many other demands on teachers' time and suggests that 'provision of teacher time generally requires additional funding at least in the short term'. Within school design projects, this issue of funding becomes particularly relevant for the senior teachers with on-going management roles, and generally some sort of secondment arrangement is implemented. It is worth noting, however, that rebuilding budgets do not include finance dedicated to this purpose and, as a result, the seconded time does not usually add up to as much as the half-time secondment recommended by Parnell. Also, this provision of costed time often does not extend to less senior teachers. If the involvement of other teachers, beyond their attendance at an initial consultation event, is valued it will be worth the school or local authority considering how an on-going commitment of time by a wider pool of teachers might be paid for.

An ultimately more intractable problem for the involvement of teachers in school design is the sense many designers and architects have of the inherent conservatism of teachers. As we have seen this is sometimes assumed to be a problem with any adult users, but it seems that at least some designers find many teachers particularly close-minded and reluctant to change their physical setting. It was this perception that led the architects of the 1960s to seek out particularly innovative teachers with whom to discuss and plan how the school environment could better support 'progressive' teaching methods. Similar assumptions about the inevitable conservatism of classroom teachers appear to be part of current school building. For example, architect and BSF facilitator, John Mitchell reports that, '[h]eadteachers frequently mistrust their staff and underestimate their capacity for creativity and innovation – as one head told me "there's little point involving the teachers, they are notoriously conservative and only interested in the size of their classrooms and where their desk is'" (Mitchell, 2008: 244). As noted previously, a clear disadvantage of only working with innovators is that ideas about typical practice become skewed. Furthermore, it seems less likely that teachers left out of a design process will be able or willing to adapt their teaching once they are managing the new or altered environment, potentially making any unexamined conservatism more entrenched. This reasoning, together with the suggested solutions of involvement and education, is evident in the writing of some architects and designers (e.g. Horne-Martin, 2006; Dudek, 2000).

It must be questioned, however, whether the reservations of teachers might sometimes be legitimate. In the case of open plan primary classrooms, there were real problems of acoustics and noise travelling, which had not been adequately addressed through design or organisational adjustments. Further, if it is accepted that teachers might sometimes foresee genuine difficulties with a design idea, then it is necessary that the process allows for such disagreement, rather than simply interpreting it as conservatism or lack of understanding of the built environment. I have written elsewhere of a project with which our research centre was involved, where teachers trying to work with a classroom design innovation became increasingly frustrated with problems that were not satisfactorily resolved, and finally avoided using the new space. Although the teachers were initially enthusiastic, they came to feel that their students' learning was being compromised by the time and effort taken up with trialling and improving the new setting:

> Apparent within the teachers' perspective, however, was a tension between the trialling and prototyping of new furniture and the teaching and learning of students, many of whom sat public examinations at the end of the school year. The level of impact on teaching and learning of an environment which takes a long time to set up and which frequently suffered technical problems should not be underestimated. The teachers nevertheless persevered for nearly two terms using the 360° classroom before a decision was made by the majority of the team to step back from the project:
>
> 'It felt to me as a teacher that I was doing a lot of work and doing extra, doing my best and all the time I was hitting obstacles and hitting brick walls and because it was just before the exams I thought, that's it I've had enough.'
>
> 'I wouldn't say it's wrecked, but it's severely disadvantaged my boys' progress because I spent so much time messing around trying to make things work.
>
> Woolner *et al.*, (2007b)

It would appear vital then that the design process is genuinely collaborative, with the differing perspectives and opinions of all participants being valued. There needs to be space and time for dialogue, where legitimate concerns based on current experience can be discussed properly and solutions found, which will probably involve flexibility both of design and of school practices. Any tendencies to conservatism by teachers, or other school staff, should not be dismissed out of hand, since this recognition and understanding of current ways of doing things is surely part of linking the new school environment to its past. This seems particularly important when a school building is to be completely replaced. Historians of education have written about the importance for a school community of a sense of continuity and shared wisdom (e.g Burke, 2007), and the knowledge of the staff, including the teachers, is clearly a central aspect of such understanding.

There is good evidence, I think, that a key challenge to teacher involvement in collaborative school design is not the particular reluctance of teachers to change their practice, but the clash of professional cultures which is sometimes evident in such projects. More generally, there is often a tension when creative people are placed in an institutional setting with which they are not familiar, often with the expectation that they will inject new ideas. This can sometimes be a great success, with gains in knowledge on both sides. For example, Goulding (2007) describes a project where artists felt they had developed their teaching skills and teachers felt they had expanded their appreciation of art as well as developing specific practical skills. Yet on other occasions, the incoming professional is frustrated by constraints and restrictions they do not understand, while the 'insiders', used to working within the familiar structure, get exasperated with the 'outsiders' for being insensitive or awkward. When interviewing artists and teachers involved in a project to include artists in BSF, I was struck by how reasonable were the complaints on both sides, but how intractable the emerging problems became. Similar experiences were noted in a project where artists worked with people on probation. Although in many ways the project was successful, the artists and the probation officers reported clashes of assumptions and expectations (Walker & Clark, 2000).

School design projects that are pursued collaboratively have the potential to avoid some of these difficulties, since neither group of professionals are being expected to immerse themselves in the setting of the other group. There are still likely to be tensions, however, caused by lack of understanding, and perhaps lack of respect for, the professional knowledge of other participants. I have discussed how this might be displayed by design professionals towards teachers, but as designers and architects have noted, there can be a parallel problem of teachers failing to understand the business of design. In their work considering the collaborative design of school grounds, Sheat and Beer talk of 'bridging the gap between educationists and designers' (Sheat & Beer, 1994: 90). This problem is also often described as being due to differing languages spoken within professional groups. Till is quite critical of this aspect of professional knowledge in architecture, claiming that 'to establish the inviolate credentials of the profession the architectural knowledge base, and its inscription in language and drawn codes, became more remote from the needs and comprehension of the users' (Till, 2005: 31). Less critically, but still recognising this problem, Parnell's interviewees 'suggested that there are issues regarding the languages used in distinct professional areas and difficulties around creating a common language dealing with design, construction and learning/pedagogy. This implies a particular roles for facilitators and challenge to be overcome before dialogue can be established' (Parnell *et al.*, 2008: 221).

As an alternative, or perhaps an addition, to Parnell's ideas about facilitators and a common language, research suggests a role here for more visual methods of consultation and communication. These can circumvent the need for professional vocabulary and provide something concrete for all participants to look at, manipulate and discuss. Creating or referring to photographs and plans can be a valuable way to understand an existing physical environment as a first step to change or development (Woolner *et al.*, 2008; 2010; Hartnell-Young & Fisher, 2007; Clark, 2005).

It must be acknowledged, however, that such methods may be resisted if participants feel that they are obstructing them in getting their point of view across. This might be a particular problem for teachers faced with more visual or spatial activities, but who feel that their professional understanding is inextricably linked to the language they usually use to express themselves. I have discussed elsewhere how some teachers involved in an initial consultation resisted a diamond ranking exercise using photographs, insisting instead on their verbal comments being recorded (Woolner *et al.*, 2010). Other researchers have described related problems with teachers using lots of words when they were invited to draw diagrams or pictures to represent their experiences (Varga-Atkins & O'Brien, 2009).

Overall there are probably no easy answers here. Among all the school users who should be participating in the design process, the successful, as opposed to the tokenistic, involvement of a good range of teachers is particularly challenging. The relative ease of finding a sample, their clearly defined professional expertise and their usual willingness to voice their opinions must not distract facilitators from the very real difficulties of finding time and appropriate methods for their full and continued participation. If the issues described in this section can be acknowledged and resolved, however, the potential prize is a school environment that accommodates current practice, but supports development, and is considered by teachers to be an integral part of educational activities.

Parents

Over the past 40 years, it is possible to identify a thread of interest in supporting and increasing the involvement of parents in the education of their children. The particular form of this concern has changed over the years, but it is still possible to see continuities. 'Community' schools established by local education authorities in the 1970s were intended to centre a school securely in its community partly through being more inclusive of, and responsive to, parents. This developed in the 1980s and 1990s into a more individualised understanding of education (Vincent, 1993), and is most recently to be seen in the intentions of proponents of 'extended schools' to integrate education into the wider provisions made for families. Most relevant to the current context, parents are not named among the parties who are supposed to be consulted during a BSF project, but would seem to be included in the requirement to consult 'the wider community' (DfES, 2002: 63). Furthermore, parents would seem to have a particularly valuable, distinct perspective, being less involved in the day to day running of the school but with a definite interest in decisions made.

Considering the requirements of school-based innovation or change, a book published at the height of experimentation with open-plan settings and 'progressive' teaching methods, proposed that 'there must be extensive involvement of the parents in the planning as well as in the implementation of the programs; otherwise, the new school is doomed before it is even opened' (IDEA, 1970: 20). Yet both research and anecdotal evidence suggest that parents are generally not involved in decisions made at the school or LA level, particularly when these decisions concern secondary education (Vincent, 1993; Thomson, 2007). The reasons for this relative lack of involvement are various, but Thomson refers to 'a substantive body of international literature which documents problems in parent-school relations' (2007: 24). There will certainly be tensions in the relationships that school staff have with parents if they come to understand the students' homelives as being the cause of difficulties in school, and school education as potentially saving them from their backgrounds. Perhaps school staff should bear in mind that some educational research has revealed that the assumptions teachers make about deficiencies in their pupils due to their up-bringing are not always supported by more objective measures (see, e.g. Fisher & Larkin, 2008).

Issues to consider when involving parents

Some of the challenges to involving parents in a school design process can be understood as particular cases of more general issues which have already been discussed. Thus there may be difficulties in parents holding somewhat dated views about education, based on their own school experience, or seeming resistant to change. As has been argued above, however, in connection with the involvement of teachers, these can be seen as being balanced by potential of parents to provide a 'long view' connecting past and future experience in the school, in a way that their children will find more difficult.

There are also issues relating to the representation of parents, some of which parallel the concerns raised over how students are chosen for involvement in projects. Acknowledging the risk of the design process becoming exclusive, the School Works Toolkit recommends the inclusion of parents, 'including those who find it difficult to get to the school' (Seymour, 2001: 29). Since the parents who become active participants in a design project are even more likely than students to be self-selected, the issues previously discussed of noticing whose voices are being listened to need to be considered. A particular aspect of the way the involvement of parents is perceived is the tendency for parents with specific interests or concerns to be sidelined as ""activist parents" ... [and so] no longer "genuine parents"' (Vincent, 1993: 238). Of course in the context of a design project, it might be quite frustrating if a subgroup of parents continue to return to a particular, perhaps seemingly unrelated, issue. Yet the demands of genuine collaboration mean that such issues should be seen as part of the parental experience and open to debate, not swept aside as irrelevant or as coming from less 'authentic' voices.

This relates to another potential tension to the involvement of parents: their knowledge and understanding of the current whole school experience is inevitably more limited than that of other potential participants. This might appear especially clear to those participants who work within the school and could lead to some irritation if parents appear to be making judgments based on misunderstandings or partial knowledge. Although frustrations might result, it seems important that a wide participatory process attempts to accommodate different experiences and expand the knowledge of those involved to include an appreciation of the experiences of other participants. Practical ways of facilitating this integration of understandings might include careful scrutiny of groupings adopted throughout the process, so that knowledge is shared, though, as mentioned previously, decisions in this area need to include consideration of power and status, so certain voices are not simply lost or over-whelmed.

A final issue relevant to the involvement of both parents and the wider community is the difficulty sometimes experienced in reaching them in sufficient, or representative, numbers. Unlike the other school users, they are not conveniently located inside the school, available to be timetabled into events as desired. More discussion will be given to this issue in the section below which considers the involvement of the wider community, but it is worth noting that the perspectives of both parents and community members may form part of the experience of some members of the school staff. It is to the inclusion of staff members beyond the teachers that I now turn.

School staff other than teaching staff

The architects and facilitators interviewed by Parnell and colleagues referred to their sense of involving school users who had not expected to be invited to contribute (see e.g. the quote from Parnell *et al.*, 2008:215 in the opening section of this chapter). Yet despite this concern with inclusion, the authors of this article and the facilitators they interviewed appear to consider that a school community only consists of teachers and students. This perspective neglects not just the parents and wider community beyond the school gate, but also the substantial number of adults working in the school in positions other than direct teaching jobs. Their roles range from those centring on personal involvement with students, such as learning supporters, mentors, teaching assistants and lunchtime supervisors to those which involve managing aspects of the school facilities, such as technicians, administrators and cleaners. This group of people tend to make up approximately a third of the school workforce, so could easily amount to fifty or sixty people in a secondary school. Their numbers have increased considerably in the last decade (Blatchford *et al.*, 2007) are likely to continue to grow, given the current tendency to a more 'extended' provision in British schools. In existing schools, it is likely that there is a large and varied non-teaching staff, as well as links to professionals based outside the school who visit the premises in their work with students and families.

For democratic reasons alone, it seems vital that these individuals are not left out of a participative design process. The fact that they are often missed out may make them pleasantly surprised to be included, but perhaps will not help them to be constructively critical within a collaborative process. Echoing the reaction of teachers reported by Parnell's facilitators, we found that school cleaners were particularly pleased to be asked to participate in an initial consultation on school redesign. It appeared that the relatively low status of their jobs in the school made it less likely that they would be invited to share their experiences and knowledge. In this connection, it is appropriate to mention the findings of work aimed at improving school breaktimes through the professional development of lunchtime supervisors. One researcher points out the benefits of a whole school approach to any training or innovation, including the observation that 'shared training also makes a statement about the status of supervisors in the school community' (Sharp, 1994:123). Echoing Jean Ruddock's experience with reluctant students, another researcher considering lunchtime supervisors adds that 'those who feel most powerless can exert a form of negative power in the form of sabotage' (Fell, 1994: 143). In a way that parallels the conclusions drawn above about the participation of students, it would seem that there are both positive and negative reasons for ensuring that school staff members from across the range of roles and jobs are included in a collaborative design process.

It is important, however, that inclusion of these staff members does not become merely a tokenistic exercise, ticking off the involvement of someone from each employment group. It must be recognised that a desire for the involvement of people from across the school staff is not just a matter of decency, politeness or reducing negative attitudes, but should result from an appreciation of their wide ranging experiences of the school. Some of these staff members will have particular, perhaps unusual or very detailed, understandings of certain aspects of the school's functioning. These perspectives include some that are fairly obvious, such as the knowledge of the kitchen staff about the catering facilities or the librarian's understanding of the school library and resource centre. In a school rebuilding project that I have been following, the knowledge and ideas of the caretaker were central to the design of the security system and procedures for the new building. Some knowledge, however, is less predictable: the school cleaners involved in our consultation provided detailed information about the resilience of all sorts of fixtures and fittings, which could guide decisions about finishes and design details in the new school premises. This suggests incidentally the importance of the continued inclusion of non-teaching staff as the design process progresses.

Even where the nature of the person's role makes their area of expertise reasonably predictable, their actual understanding can be wider or more nuanced than might be expected. Science technicians we spoke to had a complex knowledge of the circulation issues in the science block due to their movement between rooms with equipment. As a result, they had developed detailed ideas about how the science classrooms needed to be arranged and linked, and the placing of storerooms, to facilitate efficient and safe use. These descriptions of problems and proposals for improvements tended to concur with the experiences of the science teachers. Yet the ideas of the technicians were both more precise, pinpointing particular difficulties, and more complete, considering organisation and movement within the science block as a whole.

This sort of overview, resulting from the particular responsibilities of a job within the school, was not an isolated instance. During this consultation we were also struck by the overarching understanding of the school's layout, organisation and functioning held by members of the administration team. In particular, one long-serving administrator was able to discuss variations in school policies, access arrangements and timetabling, referring back over a twenty-five year span of experience. The spatial, as well as historical, reach of her knowledge was clear when she sketched her typical day on a plan of the school (see Figure 5.3 for this map and Figure 5.4 for a map produced by a teacher). Unlike many of the teachers, whose days centred on limited spaces where they usually taught, her role took her around the school, providing knowledge of particular areas, but also of how they fitted together and contributed to the functioning of the school. Thus the use of mapping was a successful activity in eliciting ideas from this participant, and helped her refer to particular places, but also made the experience on which she based her conclusions clear.

The length of service of this particular employee also highlights another quality that non-teaching staff are likely to bring to a collaborative design process: their knowledge of the school's past. As has been previously discussed, the inclusion of 'long views' is an advantage of involving any adults in the design process. The continued involvement of non-teaching staff in the life of the school as it adapts to its new setting make the participation of these people, together with the teachers, important in the linking of past, present and future use. In addition, the past experience of the non-teaching staff is particularly likely to extend beyond their current role. These staff may have changed jobs within the school and are considerably more likely than the teachers to live nearby and so have experience of the school as parents or grandparents, neighbours, or even, previously, as students themselves. Thus their knowledge of the life of the school may go back some distance in time but also be broader than initially realised. The potential insights into a wider community perspective on the school might be particularly valuable if the involvement of community members without existing connections to the school proves hard to arrange.

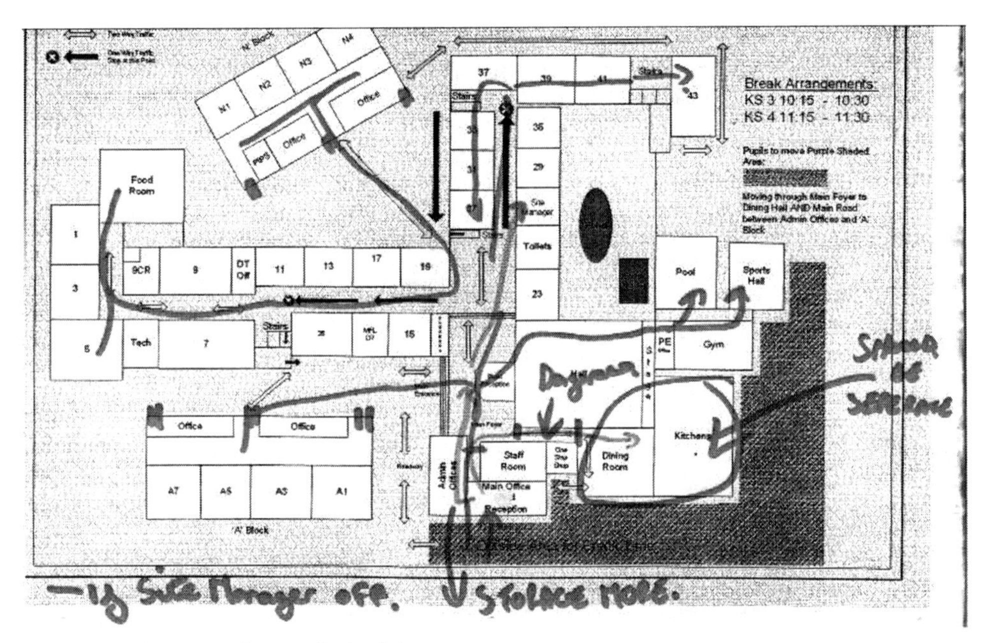

Figure 5.3 Administrator's map of school day

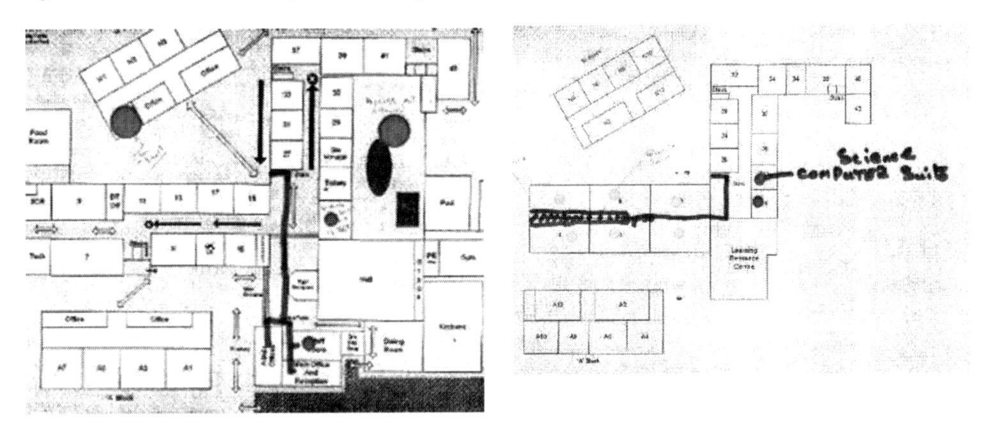

Figure 5.4 Teacher's map of school day

Issues to consider when involving other school staff

Many of the issues likely to arise over the inclusion of people from across the school staff echo challenges already discussed in connection with other groups of participants. The potential for difficulties due to differences in power and status has been considered in relation to students working side by side with adults, particularly their teachers. It has been pointed out, however, that discomfort due to power differentials could also be present in groupings of teachers. The inclusion of other staff adds to this potential problem, but perhaps also makes it more complex since some of the staff members, though in relatively poorly paid or low status jobs, may wield considerable power within limited areas. Examples might include the caretaker, the kitchen manager, the school office manager (in a small school) or a senior administrator (in a larger school). As has been discussed previously, the aim of the process must be for genuine dialogue and collaboration, but sometimes that might be furthered more effectively by relatively homogenous groupings where participants feel comfortable and confident. Such groupings during initial activities might help to develop trust in the proceedings and facilitate more mixed groupings at a later stage.

The sort of activities which are used also seems important in this respect. As has been argued previously, a mediating activity can break down barriers and build confidence, giving participants something to do initially and something to refer to as discussions proceed. During the school design consultation we facilitated, and through other research use of these tools, we have been impressed by how the provision of a structured activity helps participants to relax and begin to reveal their experiences. One advantage of using broadly visual activities, based on photographs or plans, is that participants can easily talk as they look, sort, draw or cut out. These activities did seem to be especially effective, however, in drawing out certain aspects of the specialist knowledge of the non-teaching staff. In particular, the mapping exercises were very successful in revealing the organisational understanding of certain staff members. An alternative technique, when the locations and activities of a participant during the day are of interest, involves respondents being reminded by mobile phone messages at intervals throughout the day to record where they are and what they are doing (Riddle & Arnold, 2007). These could be transposed onto a plan of the school. Having annotated plans, produced by either method, to refer to later in the design process could also be useful for establishing the validity of certain viewpoints or ideas, and so perhaps assisting in more respectful and genuine dialogue between participants of differing status who have different perspectives or understandings.

Such continued involvement of a wide range of staff members seems important to the success of the design process, as has been suggested for other groups of participants. As for other participants, it is necessary to ensure that time is made available for this, which could present particular challenges for some staff. Some of these roles, unlike that of teacher do not automatically include expectations of meetings, discussions and reflections on the job. In the work with lunchtime supervisors, it was noted that a training course for these members of staff usually provided 'the first time that lunchtime organisers had ever had the opportunity to sit down all together to think about their work' (Fell, 1994: 136). In addition to these issues relating to the cultures of certain jobs, it is also necessary to consider practical aspects, such as fitting sessions around the times staff members work or ensuring that hourly paid staff are paid for the time they contribute.

All these provisions should then make it possible for members of the school staff to contribute their wide-ranging experiences and knowledge to the design process. If these ideas are to form part of a more complete understanding of the school as currently used and inform a genuinely collaborative design process for the future school, however, they need to be integrated into the developing understanding of the school. This will involve relating a wide range of experiences and viewpoints, and it is the very diverse and disparate perspectives of the wider staff body which might make this particularly challenging. The wide range of experiences and understandings likely to be produced by the full staff of a school potentially provide a more comprehensive understanding of the school, but also make an overview more difficult to achieve.

Difficulties in participants understanding eachothers' viewpoints or experiences may sometimes be due to 'clashes of values', as was found between teachers and lunchtime supervisors discussing school breaktimes (Fell, 1994:136). In this context, a solution seemed to depend on there being genuine value given to the experience and knowledge of the lunchtime supervisors, which in turn was more likely in schools committed to a whole school approach to change. There are also echoes here of the tensions often observed between educationalists and design professionals, which were discussed in the section on teacher involvement in the design process. Again, the answer seems to include mutual respect and genuine dialogue. There are also perhaps opportunities for facilitators who are outside the particular contrasting perspectives, and for activities which produce tangible products which can form the basis of discussions or validate viewpoints.

It is worth noting, however, that sometimes there might not be a simple overview which can easily reconcile all the points of view, or a way to resolve who is right and who mistaken. This was alluded to during the earlier discussion of apparently conservative teachers whose reluctance to change their practice might relate to their understanding of education and the pressures of their role, as much as to their ignorance of the physical environment. The most pertinent example I have encountered, though, of this problem of conflicting experiences and desires belongs in the current section on the inclusion of non-teaching staff. During the consultation on school design that we facilitated, the cleaners were consistent and determined in their opposition to carpeting in the school, due to the difficulty and time involved in cleaning carpets. Yet carpets are usually agreed by students, teachers and other staff in the classroom to enhance the school experience through making the school quieter and more calm, as well as conveying expectations of sensible behaviour and so a sense of dignity to students. It is even possible to produce research evidence for the benefits of carpeting: the carefully studied American elementary school renovation project mentioned in earlier chapters included the provision of new carpets as an integral part of the refurbishment (though the project was sponsored by the US Carpet and Rug Institute! See Berry, 2002). From our conversations with the cleaning staff, however, it seemed very unlikely that they would be persuaded by any evidence or opinion to welcome carpets. However this conflict is ultimately resolved, it will not be possible to please everyone. If it is conducted well, the participatory design process should enable the various participants to appreciate other viewpoints, even if they continue to disagree with them. The danger, of course, is that the eventual resolution of this, and perhaps other more subtle and difficult to define, conflicts causes some participants to feel that their experiences are being undervalued and their opinions ignored. Again the motivation for the collaborative process, together with the details of how it is conducted, need to be scrutinised.

The wider community

In previous eras, schools have often been quite isolated from the surrounding local community. For example the design of post war secondary schools, set apart in large areas of playing fields, made them seem very separate from the nearby houses. Architectural historian Andrew Saint comments, 'the suburban secondary schools of the 1950s tended to appear marooned in an undifferentiated expanse of playing field' (Saint, 1987: 132). As discussed above in relation to the involvement of parents, however, there has been recent pressure from various policies and initiatives to integrate schools with the communities they serve. This is most obvious in connection with the extended schools agenda, but it is also evident, for instance, in the stated aims of Every Child Matters (DfES, 2004b: 9). These are considerably wider than the academic objectives of traditional schooling and suggest schools should be part of a multifaceted community in which children develop.

Against this background, it is not surprising to find recommendations that school design projects involve the local community. The consultations of a BSF project are supposed to include 'all potential users in the community' (DfES, 2002: 63) and the School Works Toolkit recommends involving the local community 'including those who haven't traditionally been involved with the schools' (Seymour, 2001: 29). While these seem laudable aims, it must be acknowledged that it will be difficult to involve in a school design process those without existing links to the school. Yet the need to do so is suggested by the conclusion drawn from the investigation of iconic schools in Chapter 1. Although the schools are very different, there was evidence of each being embedded within its local community. The wider community is also central in linking the renewed school to its past, which is considered to be important.

Once it is accepted that the involvement of the local community is worthwhile, the best ways to reach them will probably depend on the context of the school. Schools which already house shared community resources, such as sports or drama facilities, or provide extended school services, such as adult evening classes or holiday activities for children, will presumably start from these in their attempts at outreach. As discussed above, many non-teaching staff will be members of the local community, so it might be beneficial to include them in any event aimed at the wider community. Could they be encouraged to invite friends, family or neighbours as a means of widening the participant base?

Issues to consider when involving the wider community

As we have seen, there is a clear, and reasonable, desire to widen participation beyond those already involved with the school, yet these community members will probably be hardest to reach. This issue of a wide sample of local people, representative of all in the community, will therefore be the main challenge to the successful involvement of the wider community. This difficulty of sampling, however, has surfaced in connection with various groups of potential participants, particularly students and parents, and we have seen that there are no easy solutions.

A potentially more serious problem which might be encountered when involving the wider community in a school design process is that their knowledge and experience of the current premises is likely to be quite limited, and possibly out of date. Most importantly, the needs and desires of some people is also likely to be limited by their immediate connection to or use of the school: certain individuals might only want to discuss the provision of a swimming pool in the new school or the height of the building overlooking their houses. A possible solution here is to encourage the intervention of those community members with broader experience of school life, perhaps through working at the school or being parents. This could be achieved by judicious forming of groups or working parties, maybe also including students. If these people, with their wider perspectives, also think that the swimming pool or drama studio must be central to the new school, however, it might be time to concede that the single-minded locals have a point.

Concluding thoughts

The sections of this chapter have suggested the complications and conflicts which are possible, or even likely, when a wide range of individuals attempt to integrate their perspectives and opinions during a collaborative school design process. I have also tried to show, however, why these tensions are worth encountering, and discussed some general approaches to understanding and, perhaps, resolving them. As will have become clear through this and the previous chapter, there are numerous books, articles and 'toolkits' in various forms, which offer ways to organise collaborative design and activities to develop ideas. It seems possible to pursue these ideas thoroughly, reaping the benefits of the experiences of others and allowing their suggestions to enhance or inspire the development of an appropriate and useful range of methods for a particular school design project. Equally, however, it seems possible to go through the motions of participation, apparently following the suggestions of the toolkits, without people feeling truly involved. It was argued in Chapter 4 that the key to real participation lies in an ongoing, respectful and genuine dialogue, involving a wide range of people and ideas. This chapter has considered how this might broadly work in practice with a range of participants, aiming to provoke questioning and further thought, rather than offer a check list of procedures.

If this seems unsatisfactory, then I suggest that the conclusions drawn in relation to collaborative approaches to improving school breaktimes have a much more general application (Sharp & Blatchford, 1994). From their own work in this area and the research of others into breaktime behavior, school grounds and lunchtime supervision, Sharp and Blatchford reach three main conclusions about how collaborative approaches in schools can succeed. They argue firstly for the need for a holistic approach, considering all aspects of the breaktime situation, including the physical space, together with the management and organisation of time, space and people. Any change must recognise and encompass all these aspects; otherwise it will be short-lived and superficial. Similarly, it has been argued here in the more general context of school design that the physical setting cannot be seen in isolation from the activities which take place there. This complex relationship, and the potential for the transformation of education through changes to the physical space, will be further explored in the following chapters.

More clearly relevant to the foregoing discussion of collaborative design is the second conclusion about breaktimes: that for attempts at change to succeed they must involve the whole school community. The authors note that the phase 'whole school approach' is over-used but they emphasise that there is a central 'need to involve all in a meaningful dialogue about change' (Sharp & Blatchford, 1994: 190). As has been argued at some length, this conclusion deserves to be applied to our understanding of any school design process, as well as informing actual practice more than appears to be happening at present. Notably, within BSF, facilitator John Mitchell has recently concluded from his experiences that one of the main requirements for success is 'whole school involvement' (Mitchell, 2008: 244–245).

Finally, in connection with making changes to school breaktimes, it is concluded that it is important to understand that the process of change is not straightforward. Similar conclusions can be drawn from Pat Thomson's recent review of whole school change (Thomson, 2007), and the recognition that managing change in a school is not a simple task might seem fairly obvious to anyone involved in education. In the context of school design, it seems necessary for all those involved to acknowledge this, and it might seem harder to achieve such understanding if more people are involved. It must be hoped that through their involvement they come to recognise this complexity of the situation as inevitable, rather than as a failing of the particular process with which they are involved. Again the best way to achieve this aim must be through genuine collaboration, where the difficulties, as well as the successes, are seen as the shared responsibility of all parties, rather than as the result of individual power-play or willfulness.

6

Rebuilding your school: can we transform learning through space and facilities?

Introduction

So far this book has considered a number of ways of trying to establish 'what works' in school design. This has included looking at how a sample of notable schools have been adapted and evaluated over time, which provided a sense of how big ideas in architecture and education interact with each other, and with educational practice in schools. Having taken this broad brush approach to understanding school design, the next chapters attempted to investigate the separate elements of the physical environment. This revealed the aspects of the school setting which, if inadequate seem very likely to have negative impacts on the people who use it. What emerged as much more difficult, however, was to explain how to fine-tune a basically adequate environment to provide an excellent setting for learning. It was then argued that, given continued disagreement and lack of resolution about what constitutes a good educational environment, the solution must lie in designing an environment that fits the particular purposes of its users. In order to achieve such fit between the past, current and future uses of the building, it was then concluded that a participatory design process would be necessary. The previous two chapters have considered the reasoning and practical issues behind this idea, arguing for the importance of genuine dialogue and a collaborative approach, where the development of a shared understanding of the complex, dynamic relationship between the physical setting and the wide range of people who use it is central.

Thus we have arrived at a point where we have a good background understanding of school environments and of participatory design. Yet the motivation school users have for getting involved in planning their new school is generally a desire to improve the school setting, changing things for the better. If they do not think such positive change is at least a possibility, it seems unlikely that they will contribute the time and energy required a by a participatory design process. It is also this relative optimism and openness to new ideas which make the occasion of physical change a good opportunity for reflection and moving on. Change, though, in any big organisation is difficult, and the possibility and history of change in education reflects this challenge. Educationalists have grappled with this in theory (e.g. Thomson, 2007; Fullan, 2001), while practitioners and researchers often struggle with these problems in practice (e.g. Rudduck, 1980; Ouston *et al.*, 1991; Pollard, 1985; 2008)

The following chapters will consider the possibilities and practicalities involved in making alterations to the physical setting from the perspective of understanding and effecting educational change at the school level. The intention is to examine what can be done, and what is in fact being done through the current wave of redesign, to alter or improve the learning experience provided in schools. This will begin by looking at the transformation agenda associated with recent and ongoing school rebuilding projects.

The transformation agenda

Policy and theory

The announcements and proposals made about school facilities by the recently elected Labour government around the turn of the millennium tended to include a flavour of radical change and new departures. The central motivation for the developing building programme was the physical deficiencies of a stock of school buildings, particularly in the secondary sector, which were well past their intended life spans, often under-maintained or dilapidated, and needed bringing up to standard or replacing. Yet the talk was not of mundanely rebuilding schools or decorating premises but of transforming education. This is stated clearly in Building Bulletin 95, which set out the government's objectives for forthcoming capital investment and described how these school building projects should proceed. BSF was to be understood as part of the government's 'major agenda for transforming secondary education' (DfES, 2002: 3).

This explicit stating of aims of change can of course be understood against the background of general cultural and social movements at this time, and there were other related reforms and initiatives within education. For example, there were various changes within what is now popularly called 14–19 education and the implementation of extended schools services in some schools. Yet the link to school design is interesting because it might not seem immediately obvious how capital spending on premises relates to big changes in the ideas and practice of education.

A clue to the reasoning here is provided by some early reactions to the increase in school building. The Design Council was very concerned that the programme would simply provide newer, cleaner versions of old-fashioned buildings, more suited to a previous age of education. Their campaign pamphlet 'From the Inside Looking Out' (Design Council, 2005) juxtaposes photographs of classrooms in 1905 and 1950 with a twenty-first century classroom and questions why there is not more difference. In his foreword to the review we carried out for the Design Council, their Learning Environments Campaign Leader of the time, Toby Greany, commented that

> as we set out on the government's massive and exciting school building programme (the problem) is that we will use evidence from the past to inform a very similar future, when what is needed is a new approach and new solutions for school design to reflect the changing needs of learning in the 21st century. [. . .] the danger is that wider policy imperatives will leave us with another generation of schools fit for the past, rather than the future.
>
> Greany, (2005: 3–4)

It must also be acknowledged that one of the conclusions we felt confident in drawing from that review was of the potential for the exploration and redesign of one's surroundings to act as a catalyst for other change:

> There is an implication in many studies that the empowering process of re-designing and taking ownership should spill over into motivation and empowerment in other areas, encouraging creativity and experimentation in curriculum, raising motivation towards academic and social goals.
>
> Woolner *et al.*, (2007a: 63)

As we have seen in the previous chapter, the facilitators and architects interviewed by Parnell and colleagues also advance this idea on the basis of their experiences with British school design projects in recent years. Architectural consultant and 'enabler', John Mitchell makes a particularly explicit statement to this effect in the conclusion to an article detailing his experience of BSF: 'If we approach BSF as a change process ... it can be an excellent catalyst for rethinking and revitalising schools and learning' (Mitchell, 2008: 251).

Thus it can be seen that as BSF took off, there were warnings about the dangers of an isolated perception of school buildings, merely rebuilding without considering their function and use, together with suggestions of the potential for using school design as a way to kick-start a process of reflection and change. This continued to be represented by talk of transforming education through a suitably imaginative and innovative approach to school buildings. The second annual report on the progress of BSF concluded that this transformation agenda was continuing to permeate the programme:

> 'The guidance provided to schools ... points to the importance of schools viewing BSF as a once-in-a-lifetime opportunity to transform the function of secondary schools through the development of 21st century buildings with teaching and learning to match
>
> PricewaterhouseCoopers, (2008: 10)

Practice

Over the last few years my impression from talking to architects, LA advisors and headteachers is that they do indeed see the BSF initiative as centring on transformation. More broadly, such people seem to accept the fundamental linking of a new or changed building with renewal in teaching, learning and the general business of school. Some enthusiastic LA officers, particularly, it appears to me, those with educational as opposed to architectural backgrounds, perceive BSF as an opportunity to overhaul radically the secondary education system in their areas. Parnell's investigation of current practice in school design processes reaches similar conclusions about the attitude at LA level:

> Representatives from local authorities who had initiated engaging stakeholders in the process were clearly committed to the opportunuities to rethinking learning with the new school buildings. This is reflected in the names for new schools, such as 'learning centres' which are replacing secondary schools in Knowsley and in Birmingham the BSF projects are part of the council's Transforming Education Programme.
>
> Parnell *et al.*, (2008: 216)

This research, however, also suggests that educationalists within schools, as opposed to those working at the LA level, feel somewhat less confident about their ability to control and reap the rewards of the BSF process. '[S]chools apparently felt that, to date the process was happening too fast and they did not have time to think about all the issues involved' (Parnell *et al.*, 2008: 217). There is other evidence for this suggestion that ideals about educational transformation, which as we have seen grew out of policy pronouncements and cultural developments, are failing to trickle down from the LA through the school management level to the classroom level. The second annual BSF report specifically addressed this issue of the influence of the transformation agenda and concludes that:

> LA BSF Managers have a clear message on educational transformation[...] A more mixed picture emerges ... of school-level understanding.... There is positive, though not unqualified, evidence about headteachers' understanding but a less encouraging picture on teacher's engagement
>
> PricewaterhouseCoopers, (2008: 16).

The reasons for this situation seem to centre, as Parnell suggests, on a sense of lack of time. John Mitchell concurs that time pressures are a particular problem with BSF, and argues that because of them some LA officers are scared off real engagement with educational change, imagining that 'we don't have the time and don't want to disrupt the programme by "setting hares running"' (Mitchell, 2008: 245). There is a sense that this might be a reflection of more general perceptions and experiences within education currently, rather than due to particular failings of the BSF programme or the wider British school building initiative. In 2001, educationalist Michael Fielding made a much more sweeping judgement about the contemporary educational culture, claiming that, 'there are too many imperatives that require 'delivery', too much that demands coverage, too little that provides the enabling condition for us to be quiet and attentive in ways that make exploration or creativity a real possibility' (Fielding 2001:103).

This has implications for BSF projects, and indeed for any time-consuming, complex investigation of ideas, such as I have argued collaborative design is centred upon. The question, of course, is how much these perceptions, generally of observers from outside the immediate school organisation, really reflect the experiences of those in school. Even if these feelings of pressure and lack of opportunity for discussion and reflection are widely experienced, it seems possible that time and space might be being found in some schools for engagement with change to the learning environment. Although the BSF report was pessimistic about the transformation agenda reaching teachers, it seems possible that many in the classroom, both teachers and other staff, are reflecting on their practice in light of changes being proposed, or enacted, on the physical and organisational environment in their school. Just because they are not using particular terms or talking as explicitly about the transformation of learning as LA officers does not necessarily indicate that they are unconcerned or unaware. In this respect, a more worrying finding from the BSF reports to date is the relative lack of involvement of classroom teachers and other staff in the BSF design processes in schools (PricewaterhouseCoopers, 2007; 2008). The 2008 evaluation survey of headteachers in BSF schools found that heads reported the involvement of themselves and their deputies but less than a fifth described a classroom based member of staff as being 'involved or likely to be involved' in the BSF process.

Difficult though it is to quantify how much time, or other evidence of involvement, is 'enough', it is concerning if people across the school community do not seem to be or feel themselves to be part of the process. This undermines the ideal of collaborative design and threatens the fundamental aim of development occurring through users understanding the school setting and their contribution to it. This would seem to constitute a real threat to any hopes of transformation within education.

Engaging with physical change to learning environments

It would seem then that there are some problems with the official transformation agenda and, in particular, with the opportunity, ability or willingness of actors in the actual school setting to engage with it. How then should people with involvement in schools approach understanding or changing their environments? Perhaps there is room here for activity from the bottom up, which originates in experiences within the existing setting rather than through imposed over-arching ideas about educational transformation. We have seen from history, particularly the experience of 'progressive' primary education in the 1960s, that there is no inevitability about transformation or change in education, even, or perhaps especially, when it is mandated from above. So, perhaps we should not be too disappointed or surprised if the transformation agenda of policy and theory fails to be recognised in everyday practice in schools. If the solution then is to move away from this idea of all-encompassing transformation to a recognition of a more iterative, even piecemeal, approach, what parts of the complex interaction of people and place which constitutes a school are most open to useful grassroots development and change?

Although I have argued that an understanding of the school learning environment cannot be reduced to simple physical building blocks of school premises, it seems likely that there are parts of the school's design, management and use where change will have more impact on the learning and teaching experience. Although, as I have argued, it is important to understand your school as a complex interaction of setting and behaviour, which cannot simply be reduced to a physical environment, this does not necessarily mean that we always have to consider the complete school. Instead it should be possible to focus on the relationship between the people and the surroundings in particular areas of the school or aspects of school life. Although these will be set within the larger dynamic of the school as a whole, it will be helpful to take a more focused approach so that the energy, time and expertise of the participants in the design process can be used most effectively and efficiently. Therefore, in the sections that follow, I will be considering parts of the school environment, but these should be understood as existing within the wider setting of the whole school, and indeed as part of the educational ideas and attitudes of society. I will also be aiming to avoid a more general reduction to the purely physical, instead continuing to emphasise the importance of understanding the dynamic relationships between users and settings.

Organisation and layout of teaching and learning space

The overall arrangement

During our school design consultation, carried out in a secondary school before their BSF process began, there was a lot of quite intense discussion of overall school layout, which involved classroom teachers, sometimes senior teachers, and a range of non-teaching staff. On subsequent visits to other schools where building work was in progress or complete, I have not found this aspect of the school design being discussed, presumably because it seems too late for any new idea to be implemented. This shows the importance of time being available during initial consultations for these discussions to develop between staff from across the school. Understanding the possibilities, and then arriving at an overarching plan for organisation seems an important foundation stage, to which as many people as possible should contribute.

There were two central, linked issues debated during our consultation. These were the whether the overall plan of the school should include separate blocks or consist of only one building, and how areas for particular school subjects should be grouped and arranged. The existing arrangement of separate blocks owned by particular disciplines was appreciated for giving character to certain areas of the school and suggesting distinctiveness for the subjects. This could be interpreted as being an aid to orientation and route-finding around the school. The chief problems, however, were with fragmentation between subjects, as subject-specialist teachers tended to stay in their areas, and the practical issues of movement between blocks involving going outside. As would be expected with the range of people involved in these discussions, there was not one simple solution to this discussion. The ideas which tended to be settled upon involved distinct subject bases, but with more possibility for interaction between them. Ways suggested by staff to encourage this included resources or storage and preparation space shared between related subjects, such as humanities subjects or between mathematics and science.

Most staff and students favoured a single building, perhaps with 'fingers' to suggest separate blocks, avoiding the need to get wet or cold during movement between parts of the school. Considering the exemplar school buildings suggested by the government (DfES, 2004) and the architecture of schools currently being built or recently finished, suggests that having a single building is a popular decision. It must be noted, however, that among the staff and students we talked to, this was not a unanimous position. One member of the administartion staff described how she appreciated the chance to get some fresh air as she moved around the school and students were generally much more positive about external areas of the school than were staff. It seems a distinct possibility that, when memories of running between school blocks in the rain and doors banging in the wind have faded, school users will again begin to desire a layout which involves more direct and frequent interfaces between inside and outside areas.

Circulation

The arrangement of circulation space within a school might not appear to be an issue relevant to teaching and learning, and, in fact, we will be revisiting this aspect of school design in the next chapter dealing with issues of social space and relationships between people. It is also necessary, however,to consider circulation in connection with learning and teaching. As educators will be aware and educationalists have pointed out, problems in corridors and hallways have a habit of spreading into the classroom. For example, in their book about effective teaching, Daniel Muijs and David Reynolds write about the potential for whole school policies regarding tidiness or noise levels in corridors to improve 'classroom climate', making it more conducive for learning (Muijs & Reynolds, 2001:61). Furthermore, in a complete school rebuilding project, there will inevitably be tensions between space committed to teaching and learning, and space used for circulation and movement.

During our consultation, circulation within the existing school emerged as a clear problem, recognised as a priority across the various groups of participants. The narrow corridors were consistently pinpointed as causing difficulties at lesson changeover times, as were the organisational policies, primarily a one-way system, put in place to try to ameliorate the resulting tensions. The initial response of teachers was to demand wider corridors for the new school, but as one teacher pointed out during discussion, the space needed for wider corridors was likely to be taken from classrooms. Are corridors really so important that teachers are willing to settle for smaller teaching spaces? An interesting aside to this is that, in one recently built school that I visited, the art department had precisely this decision to make and decided to forego the corridor entirely and have entry to one classroom through another, so maximising the size of the rooms.

Sometimes it might be possible to achieve a wider corridor without encroaching on classrooms. Architect Sarah Ross, who conducted a study of corridor space in secondary schools, found one school which had, at considerable expense, built a new block with an unusually wide main corridor (Ross, 2006). I will be considering the findings of her research on this corridor more fully in the next chapter, but it is worth noting here the feelings of school staff that the expense of a wider corridor, which was not balanced by reduced teaching space, was justifiable in terms of a more positive learning environment.

Another possibility for improved corridor space which could be designed into a new building is avoiding corridors without natural light. This is currently being achieved in some new schools through central atria which light main circulation spaces, often on several levels and including staircases. This avoids the darkness or reliance on artificial light, which is inevitable in corridors with only a window or door at one end, and which adds to the experience of narrowness and restriction. Often, however, these atrium-based designs also produce a tradeoff between corridor and classroom, but of daylight rather than of space. This is because in some schools of this design, classrooms only receive their daylight via the atrium, making them distinctly dingy, especially in the winter. There can also be problems ventilating such rooms, as well as the isolating effect of not having an view to the outside from the classroom (see Figure 6.1).

A general solution to these recurring problems of tradeoffs between circulation and teaching space is to include circulation spaces which also have other uses. This avoids

Figure 6.1 Classroom with windows only onto an atrium

arguments about whether the expense, floorspace or daylight of a large circulation area can really be justified when it is only occupied in five minute bursts a few times a day. This is a design solution which has been tried in different ways at various times through the history of school buildings. In many ways very similar to the modern atrium, was the central hall design popular in British elementary board schools in the late nineteenth century (see Seaborne & Lowe, 1977 for details). These are based on classrooms opening directly off a central hall, which therefore doubles as large assembly room and circulation space. As is often claimed for the artrium design, it also made possible 'passive' surveilance, though in the nineteenth century this was mainly of unqualified teachers and pupil-monitors by the headteacher. Where these schools are still in use, there are some issues with noise travelling easily between classrooms, particularly if the hall area is used as breakout space for small groups. This problem with noise will be especially severe if classroom doors are left open to improve air circulation, which they are likely to be since inadequate ventilation was agreed over one hundred years ago to be a drawback to this design.

As described in Chapter 1, the middle years of the twentieth century saw a clear preference, in both primary and secondary schools, for self-contained classrooms, generally accessed from corridors. In the 1960s and 1970s, however, as part of the general acceptance of open plan arrangements in primary schools, there were many schemes for combining circulation and teaching space. As has been discussed previously, the wholesale conversion of primary schools to open plan faltered for a number of reasons. These included some poor designs where circulation essentially took place throughout the teaching spaces and must have made the learning experience resemble sitting on a bench in a busy highstreet. As anyone whose house includes a kitchen with an external door and entrances to other rooms will know, spaces people walk through have to be kept clear and these virtual corridors quickly reduce the useful space available in the room.

A more successful way of combining circulation and other usage of space, so avoiding over-reliance on corridors, is through using the main school hall for circulation. This use of the hall, which may also double as diningroom and sportshall, is found in primary and middle schools built throughout the twentieth century and clearly recalls the Board School central hall design. There are advantages, in terms of making productive use of more of the available space for more of the day, and the problem of noise, noted above, can be reduced through short corridors or cloakroom areas between classroom doors and the hall itself. It is only really possible in small schools, however, for there to be the communication and organisation necessary to make good use of the hall area without clashes. Even in small primary schools, there are likely to be some tensions as, for instance, PE is likely to be timetabled by most teachers for the afternoon and result in more competition for the hall at certain times. The use of hall spaces for dining can also be problematic, since this will make them inaccessible for other uses through the lunchtime, as well as for some time before and after lunch.

A possibility for combining circulation and learning space in larger schools is through breakout spaces between classrooms. These can be seen as applying the shared hall model on a smaller scale to a subset of classrooms within a bigger school. For this reason, tensions found in primary schools around the shared use of the hall are likely to be replicated in bigger schools with shared breakout space. Sometimes, these spaces are also used for dining and, again, the implications of this for other users and activities will need to be considered and discussed by all parties. A more profound problem, however, with breakout space is ensuring that it actually gets used at all. If it is not used for teaching or learning activities, then it becomes merely an over-large, and perhaps wasteful, circulation and transition space. Yet if teachers' practice is based on the use of a single classroom, they may find it hard to know how to accommodate this extra space within that practice.

A possible solution suggested by the teachers we consulted and which has been successfully implemented for secondary science classrooms (Arzi, 1998), is to design the space to contain shared resources, such as reference materials, ICT or special equipment. In more practical subjects the shared space could consist of an area for reading or writing up, while in more academic subjects, the space could be used for practical activities or teacher-led demonstrations. Such ideas, however, of designing spaces between classrooms with particular purposes, may lead to other problems, such as the security issues of having equipment stored in a fairly open and accessible place. Solving these problems, and, indeed, just the concerted use of these areas may fundamentally conflict with the original intention of combining learning space with circulation space.

Whole school resources

Some issues to do with the location and organisation of resources used by the whole school have been touched upon in the previous section. Although the discussion was focused on circulation, it became clear that, particularly in a small school, the central location of spaces used by all can be convenient and efficient. This becomes more complicated in larger schools and in secondary schools with more specialist facilities, particularly if these are to double as community facilities.

A common solution to accommodate sports facilities, which will be open outside school hours, is build the sports centre at one end of the school building so it can be open in isolation from the rest of the school. This has a tendency, though, to convey a sense that sport and exercise are somewhat peripheral to the life of the school. A more acceptable solution might be to group the sports facilities, together with other areas which may be open at times to the public, at the front of the school as part of its public face, with the more private classrooms, storerooms and offices forming the rear of the school premises. This general approach to the layout of the school can also be appropriate for accommodating facilities, such as a library, which might be used by the school and the wider community at the same time. In one twenty-first century secondary school, where I have carried out research work, the school library is also the local public library, which involves separate entrances for the school users and community users, and swipe card technology, but which is considered to be worthwhile and generally successful. The advantages for social interactions and the relationship of the school to its community will be further described in the next chapter.

As this example of a community-used library suggests, the location and design of shared learning and teaching resources such as the library and ICT suite involves questions both of physical structure and of timetabling and organisation. Is it the intention that such resources should be fairly freely available to all staff and students through the school day? This suggests a central location, or perhaps having the resoures spread across the school in several locations. It also implies a fairly large, perhaps somewhat open design, for these spaces, maybe including overflow areas for when the main space gets crowded. This has clear implications for staffing, which need to be considered. If on the other hand, the intention is to timetable the use of these resource areas, or operate a booking system, then the location of these spaces becomes less important and they can probably be smaller. If their main users will be whole classes superrvised by a teacher, this reduces the need for specialist non-teaching staff, but will increase the need for the spaces to be quite self-contained and generally designed to faciliate traditional, didactic teaching rather than self-directed learning.

Classroom size and shape

As was pointed out in Chapter 1 in relation to the iconic schools of the later twentieth century, it is entirely possible for an architecturally innovative building to contain very traditional classrooms. Therefore it should not really surprise one when, inside the curved, sweeping, modern structures favoured by current school designers, one finds a run of identical, basically rectangular, self-contained classrooms. Of course there are some exceptions to this description, more in some schools than in others, but it is still interesting to examine the alternatives and consider why traditional classrooms are still being built. In particular, we should consider what this suggests for the transformation agenda, which, as we have seen, is sometimes interpreted as demanding a radical break from such traditional school infrastructure.

Considering first the shape of teaching rooms, a rectangular room is appropriate for whole class teaching, since there will be no hidden corners, but the room could equally be adapted through the arrangement of furniture and equipment for more independent learning. Rectangles also fit together easily, making the planning of sections of the school relatively simple. Some architects argue that an L-shaped classroom has all the advantages of a rectangular room, but also provides more opportunities for teacher adaptation (Dudek, 2000: 56–57). In practice, however, this shape may result in an area which the teacher cannot easily see, reducing the use that can be made of that space and perhaps leading to classroom management difficulties.

Occasionally school designs are based on rooms that are hexagonal or triangular, but this leads to difficulties with furniture. Since most furniture is based on right-angles, standard items will not fit into the corners of such rooms, resulting in wasted space. When I visited a primary school which was built in the 1970s with triangular rooms, I was struck by how strange the corners where the walls meet at less than 90° feel. This is particularly the case if you enter a triangular room through a door near such a corner, since you find yourself thrust against the other wall rather than looking into the room. Considering a more recently designed school, I talked to an architect about a secondary school on which his practice was working and where the headteacher was very keen on triangular rooms. He explained that since these rooms were to be accessed from a corridor, it was difficult to achieve adequate daylight for the alternate rooms which lay against the corridor instead of the external wall. The architects on this project seemed unconvinced over what was really being gained by the triangular rooms, suspecting the headteacher of being modish.

Moving now to the size of rooms, it is notable that a desire for various sizes for different purposes has been felt through time. Recall that at Finmere (see Chapter 1), the ability to combine and separate the three areas of the primary school producing different sized spaces was a central point of the design. As at Finmere, the means of altering the rooms is generally a folding partition, and there are virtually always problems with sound carrying through such partitions. Even if this difficulty can be solved through improved materials and construction of such partitions, there is the more fundamental problem with furnishings in the space. Furniture will need to be arranged differently when the full area is being used, compared to when the space is being used as a number of smaller rooms. This suggests a lot of reorganisation, as well as some immovable fittings, such as an IWB, that will inevitably be usefully placed for only one of the possible arrangements. As was pointed out in the 1970s and '80s in reference to open plan classrooms, this sort of apparent flexibility of setting may lead to unreasonable demands for flexibility being made on the teacher. Often, the result is that partitions are not much used, the flexibility of the space is not utilised and staff manage with standard sized classrooms.

A more logical approach to the need for different sized rooms for different purposes, at least in a large school, might be to construct rooms of various different sizes. At a school I visited during its construction, this approach is being taken in a number of subject areas, including science and food. There are double size science practical rooms for use by several classes at a time, as well as intentions for the school hall with its tiered seating to be used for showing films or lecture-style presentations to large numbers of students. The success of this design, however, will depend on how well timetabling and organisation of the use of these spaces can be organised. A food technology teacher I spoke to pointed out that for some of the teaching she does, including for example small group discussions relating to childcare courses, the double-size practical food room is inappropriate. As this aspect of the problems of providing and using flexible space makes clear, sometimes achieving an appropriate learning environment relies as much on the management of space and people as on the physical space itself.

Inside the classroom

As is evident from the previous sections, decisions made at the school or departmental level about the design of teaching space and its organisation once the new building is in use, will have implications for the ways that a teacher is able to use the classroom space. This is a point which is sometimes underemphasised by those with backgrounds in design or architecture, such Sandra Horne-Martin, who often seem overly optimistic about what teachers can do within their classrooms. The influence, either positive or negative, of decisions taken at a higher level indicate again the importance of ensuring that the design process involves a wide range of classroom staff. Only if they are involved in the decision to move to open plan classrooms or rooms of differing sizes can they be expected to embed this use of the environment within their practice, rather than react against it.

There are some parts of the school learning environment, however, which, even though they may be affected by school policies, lie squarely within the classroom itself.

Although staff in the classroom might have some misgivings about the design of the room they are using, there will be elements which fall under their control and which they can adjust to provide a better fit with the sort of learning and teaching they hope will occur. It is these features of the learning environment which will be considered next.

IWBs

IWBs are increasingly seem as a necessity in classrooms. They have steadily been added to primary classrooms and are likely to be a central part of the BSF rebuilding and refurbishments of secondary schools. Although they can be used in imaginative and innovative ways, this is not inevitable. Research in the early days of their introduction into primary schools suggested that much of their use was not actually interactive, reducing rather than increasing the time that learners themselves spend engaging with ICT. As might be expected at that stage in their introduction, there were also technical difficulties and serious deficiencies in teacher expertise (Smith *et al.*, 2005; Hall & Higgins, 2005).

As would be expected, the growing prevalence of IWBs is easing some of these initial problems. Teachers I have spoken to are much more comfortable with the technology and, within schools, ideas and applications are shared, aided by the increasing size, availability and cheapness of portable solid state memory devices. When I attended the opening night of a completely rebuilt secondary school, it was notable how often the teachers referred to the IWBs, which were in every classroom. They were clearly excited at the potential of these for teaching, suggesting that they would motivate and interest their students. Although, as was argued in Chapter 3 in relation to new technology, this enthusiasm and the cost of the devices might not be proportional to their actual utility, it seems important for a classroom teacher to engage with such developments and see how they fit within their practice. This is only really possible if staff have easy access to the technology and, in this respect, the tendency to install IWBs and perhaps other technology throughout new schools can only be seen as positive.

There are also practical issues to consider in the installation of IWBs. In primary classrooms, it may be more appropriate to place them low down on a wall, if they will generally be used by children sitting on the floor. The alternative to this, revealed by a study of the use of space in primary classrooms, is that children get very uncomfortable looking up at the IWB with this contributing to their dislike of whole class teaching on the carpet and perhaps leading to behavioural problems (McCarter, 2009). Even in secondary classrooms, where the students will be seated at desks, there can be problems in putting the IWB where it can be seen by all. In teaching rooms, such as science rooms, that include a demonstration desk, which also needs to be visible to the class, there might be competition for this space. Simply putting the IWB higher up the wall may limit interaction and result in it merely being used as a screen for projection.

Finally, although research into IWBs has indicated the importance of training for teachers, it would be unfortunate if being trained and learning to use the IWBs come to dominate the adaptation of staff to their new school building. In one school whose rebuilding I have been following, there were some suggestions from conversations with teachers that much of the inservice training time, which might have been used for wide-ranging discussions about teaching and learning in the new school environment, was being devoted to IWB training.

Furniture

Teachers are continually advised by both educationalists and architects to take a flexible approach to furniture, rearranging it to suit the style of learning and teaching they wish to occur (see e.g Horne-Martin, 2006: 94; Muijs & Reynolds, 2001: 38). As explored in Chapter 3, there is sound research evidence for the impact of furniture arrangement on the learning behaviour of students and, perhaps, on the style of teaching practiced by the teacher. So this advice to teachers has a reasonable basis, but as ever, practical issues might get in the way of acting on the advice.

The first issue is the relative ease of moving the furniture, and to improve this, designers tend to focus on the furniture itself. Classroom furniture for primary schools was developed during the 1960s which was intended to facilitate rearrangement through shapes that could be combined in different ways and a fairly light construction that made movement easier. Similarly, the designers who worked on the Design Council's 360° classroom project developed a seating system which was intended to facilitate movement and rearrangement. As was discovered during that project though, a key influence on rearranging furniture is the space available; however well-designed your furniture, if there is too much of it and too many learners packed into a small space, it will be harder to move around.

Of course there are other aspects of the school setting which also impact on a teacher's ability to rearrange the furniture. An important element is time: is there time before a lesson to rearrange a room? If not, are the lessons long enough to justify the use of the first few minutes to arrange the furniture appropriately? Ownership of the room is also very important since it might be possible for a teacher to develop an organisation of the classroom which generally suits their teaching, but then struggle to enact it in every room if they are teaching in a number of different rooms. Teachers rearranging furniture in shared spaces can lead to resentment about how rooms are left and arguments about what the default set-up should be.

Finally it is worth noting a few cases of which I am personally aware where primary school teachers have decided that school desks and chairs are best moved right out of the way or even banished from the classroom. The study mentioned above of carpet space in a primary school (McCarter, 2009) revealed one teacher whose organisation of space involved maximising the carpet space by arranging all the desks around the perimeter of the room. This provided much more floor space where she could use a range of teaching and learning approaches, allowed a better view of the IWB and resulted in happier children. In another primary school I visited, this sort of arrangement of the room had convinced the teachers that they had many more tables and chairs than was necessary for their preferred teaching style, so they planned their removal and replacement with mats and cushions.

Practical rooms

It is notable that the research into the organisation of furniture and equipment within the classroom tends to assume a generic classroom of tables and chairs, rather than a workshop or laboratory space intended for practical work. There is limited guidance and research relating to the organisation of space for science, some of which suggests alternatives to the traditional laboratory layout (Arzi, 1998). Yet, many new secondary schools seem to be being built with practical rooms which are really standard classrooms containing specialist equipment. Perhaps, given the limited nature of knowledge about alternative spatial arrangements, the solution lies in the involvement, at a very early stage in the design process, of the specialist teachers, TAs, and technicians who will be working in the rooms. Through considering the wide range of learning that goes on in these rooms, not all of which will be practical, appropriate designs for these spaces may emerge. As has been emphasised previously, the genuine involvement of these staff members might also help them to be more in tune with the eventual rooms, rather than resenting innovations which they see as imposed upon them in order to fulfil other objectives.

Concluding thoughts

This chapter has considered the potential of the current wave of school building to transform education through the effects of school design on learning and teaching. It has been argued that although these new school buildings will impact on the learning and teaching that takes place within them, it is a mistake to expect clear, consistent, predictable change in line with a national policy agenda of transformation. Instead previous experiences of change and reform in education, including change which involves the physical school environment, suggests that change can be expected to be more fragmentary and varied.

Looking in more detail at some of the elements of the new schools which might be expected to affect learning and teaching has reinforced the ideas previously developed of the school environment consisting of a dynamic interaction between setting and practice. We have seen how more complete understandings of particular aspects of the school setting need to include consideration of the intentions of the people involved, as well as management and organisation of both time and space. The most productive way to develop such understanding of a particular school environment would seem to be the involvement of a wide range of people in the processes of design and change. Through facilitating and encouraging such involvement, individual schools undergoing a rebuilding process can increase the chances of the new school premises having a positive impact on teaching and learning which goes deeper than the feel good factor associated with a shiny new building. It seems important, however, also to examine the impact that a new building will have on attitudes and social behaviours in school, and it is this aspect of a rebuilding project which will be considered in the next chapter.

7 Rebuilding your school: can we change relationships through altered social space and school organisation?

Introduction

At the end of the 1970s, in a thorough review of the evidence at the time for the physical environment affecting education, the American educationalist and environmental psychologist Carol Weinstein was cautious about a direct positive impact on student achievement. She concluded that although the 'weight of the evidence suggests that design features can have a significant influence on students' general behaviour ... and on their attitudes' (1979: 584), it is difficult to find reliable evidence of a definite effect on achievement. She pointed out, however, that the 'more positive attitudes and behaviours may eventually result in improved achievement' (1979: 599). Although other reviews (see, for example, Moore & Lackney, 1993) and more recent research (Estyn, 2007) have since suggested that there may be direct effects on learning, reflected in student performance, these are generally observed as deficits in attainment in schools with particularly poor environments. It seems likely that these direct effects are only discernible in a minority of cases, with the impact of the physical setting on learning generally being mediated through the attitudes, intentions and behaviour of students, teachers and others. This is consistent with the view developed through the present book of the school environment as a complex web of influences linking people and settings.

It is therefore important to understand the impact of a new school building on the attitudes of its users and on their social interactions and relationships. This influence will encompass both general reactions to the process of rebuilding and occupying the new school, and the effect of particular parts of the design. Current and recent school designs have certain social features in common and it will be interesting to consider their likely impact. Clearly such interest in the attitudes of the school's users indicates yet again the necessity for wide involvement in all stages of the design and building process, from initial planning through to assessment of fit as the new building comes into use. Considering the attitudes of the school users should also alert us to the negative effects of the rebuilding process, such as disruption, disorganisation and disorientation, and encourage us to think about how these might be ameliorated.

Entrances

In many of the secondary schools currently undergoing rebuilding work, explicit consideration has been given to entrances. This sometimes involves organising separate entrances for differing year groups in an attempt to provide social cohesion within year groups, and perhaps minimise opportunities for younger students to be intimidated by older students. In other schools, as mentioned in the previous chapter, the motivating factor is designing entrances for members of the public using community facilities. Yet, in all these schools, there is usually explicit thought given to the overall appearance of the main public entrance. Perhaps partly in reaction to the unassuming, even hard to find, entrances to the secondary schools built from the 1960s to the 1980s, entrances to recently built schools tend to be somewhat palatial (see Figure 7.1 for comparison).

These recently designed entrances are typically very obvious from the outside, with double or revolving doors leading off a sweeping drive or paved area. Inside, the entrance hall is generally a high-ceilinged, bright place, decorated with plants, flowers and displays of student work and achievement. This suggests a return to seeing the school as a temple to education, which might appear a somewhat nineteenth century understanding, and contrasts with the post war functionalism of simple structures for school communities to inhabit and make their own. At a time, however, when in some circles it has become acceptable to make casual condemnations of local schools, it is

Figure 7.1 Unassuming entrance to a 1970s-designed school (left) and the lofty entrance area in a recently designed school (right)

understandable if these schools want their public faces to look impressive. This was put very clearly by the headteacher of a newly opened school talking to a journalist, who asserted, 'This is more than just another school in Hackney: it is a symbolic school, an emblem, saying these places should be where children from all backgrounds in inner city areas should come and be successful' (Ward, 2004).

This achievement of symbolic space and light is sometimes at the expense, though, of more well-used parts of the school. Not only is money spent here unavailable for other parts, but the design might necessitate classrooms looking onto or through an atrium, instead of directly outside. As discussed in the previous chapter, this can produce classrooms which do not receive much daylight and are difficult to ventilate. It is paradoxical that in some newly built schools, which give a general impression of lightness and airiness, the classrooms and preparation rooms where staff and students spend most of their time are distinctly dark and stuffy.

Atria

This brings us to the feature which has come to signify a twenty-first century school: the atrium. Sometimes used for the entrance, and sometimes to enclose a central social space, these atria have become increasingly common. The potential problem with such fashionable elements is that they catch on and get incorporated into every building before their disadvantages or management implications become clear. For example, it was only once flat roofs had become ubiquitous in school buildings built through the post war period and into the 1960s, that the true scale of the challenge of repairing and maintaining them became obvious. As an indication of the scale of the reaction which followed, it is notable that by the 1980s even schools using the CLASP system, which had been based on flat-roofed structures, were being designed with pitched roofs (Saint, 1987: 181). From conversations and observations in recently built schools, it would appear that the cleaning and maintenance of atria has been somewhat addressed during the planning stages of these new schools, but their general resistance to wear will only become gradually apparent.

Their appeal seems to centre on perceptions of social needs within the school, and recent ideas for improving staff and student morale through providing bright, open spaces where behaviour can be subject to so-called passive surveillance. Again, as with school entrances, this might be seen as a reaction to what had gone before. The BSF building bulletin from the DfES notes that 'many existing schools have narrow, poorly lit corridors with low ceilings. These spaces are unattractive and lead to congestion and, in the worst cases, behavioural difficulties' (DfES, 2002, p. 28). It seems likely, however, that the new atrium spaces might just facilitate different social problems to those previously experienced. Although there may be no need for staff to police a one-way system through the atrium, they might instead need to be watching out for students spitting from overlooking balconies.

It seems possible that some of these antisocial behaviours might be minimised through a more personal, less institutional, approach to student wellbeing, and some schools have been developing new organisational models in parallel to the rebuilding process. In some schools, there are open, atrium-type spaces for each year group and the idea is to provide a spatial centre for students in each year. This might involve offices for pastoral staff with responsibilities for that year being located off the space, and regular briefings or assemblies being held there. Another scheme involves the open atrium space being used for a combination of social and more formal purposes. This could suggest to staff and students that the school is concerned about the whole child, not just with academic achievement. In practice, however, the dual use of spaces for dining and teaching, which often occurs in these areas, might have practical, as well as social, consequences. Practical considerations have been mentioned in the previous chapter and include the need to allow for preparation before and clearing up after mealtimes when timetabling the use of these areas. In addition, it might be questioned whether learners can always be relied upon to adapt quickly to the change from social time to lesson time when this is not signalled by a change of location. Certainly, it will require different techniques from staff to suggest changes in intentions, and so appropriate behaviour, when they do not have a traditional classroom to enter.

Community use of facilities

In the past, particularly in the US, much discussion of the inclusion of community facilities into schools tended to focus on the improved efficiency of sharing space and making use of school premises outside school hours. Although these ideas still surface, an important part of the current enthusiasm for shared facilities is the concern for schools to be more embedded in their communities. This is clearly a social aim, but it can seem rather abstract. Schools are being built with shared facilities but there has not been much research, or even comment, about the impact this might be having on community relations. An interesting aspect of a changed relationship between the school and its local community has been noted in one twenty-first century secondary school which I have visited. This school, as mentioned in the previous chapter, has been constructed with a library which is also the local public library. The librarians have noticed that when the library is open to the public during school time, parents sometimes use it as a way of keeping in touch with the school and their child's progress, without the need to make explicit visits or inquiries. So, in effect, the school is more welcoming to parents, but this is occurring without the explicit focus on parental involvement, which many parents, and their offspring, might find uncomfortable. It would be interesting to know how common this use of the library is in this school and how aware of it other school staff are, as well as how widespread such use of shared community facilities might be in other schools. Improved understanding of this aspect of community relations might include ideas on how to develop, or broaden, this community-wide version of passive surveillance.

Circulation space

In the previous chapter, circulation space was discussed in relation to its impact on teaching and learning, and the balance that needs to be struck between space for movement and space for learning. An aspect of this balance is the effect of cramped circulation space on the interaction and resulting relationships between students and with staff. As mentioned above, a clear lead was provided by the government that new schools should rethink their circulation space to avoid the behavioural problems associated with narrow corridors. Furthermore, any consultation with students and staff at the planning stage of the new school is likely to find that addressing the existing circulation problems will be a priority. During the participatory planning sessions that we facilitated in a secondary school, a concern over the corridors was shared by just about all participants. The mapping and the photograph based activities all revealed some consistent problems with circulation. In particular, the plan of accumulated student likes and dislikes showed hot spots of dislike along the most heavily used parts of the corridors and at intersections, stairs and doorways, and a similar pattern emerged from the maps produced by the staff. A view of a corridor in a photograph provoked telling comments from students, particularly the younger ones, and reflections from teachers on the difficulties of managing transitions pleasantly. It was clear that the narrow, rather dark, corridors were producing strained relationships and, quite often, actual confrontations.

While it may be hoped that wider corridors would reduce these tensions, it might be questioned whether the improvement will be enough to justify the resulting expense. Many of the atria based circulation systems used in newer schools would seem to be an attempt at compromise, where narrow corridors are avoided but, because the atrium space has other uses, pure expenditure on wider corridors is avoided. Occasionally, though, school communities might decide that wider corridors are a major priority and specifically target this aspect of their premises.

As mentioned in the previous chapter, architect Sarah Ross was fortunate enough to find a school which had a new block built with a wide main corridor, which she was able to compare with a similar standard-width corridor in an older block (Ross, 2006). The contrast was striking. Through various methods, students reported feeling more positive and happier in the new corridor, while teachers who were interviewed thought there were fewer behavioural problems. Research observations of behaviour and interactions in the two corridors more than supported this idea with very few instances of running, shouting or altercations in the new corridor, while many were recorded in the old corridor. The researcher was struck by how quickly incidents escalated in the constrained space of the narrow corridor, and hypothesised that it was much more possible for students to avoid confrontations in the wider corridor.

An additional finding of this piece of research, however, serves to question the passivity of passive surveillance. Although the teachers were generally very pleased with the new corridor, they did offer some criticism of one aspect of its design. This was the glass paneling between the classrooms and the corridor, which they found made them responsible for policing the corridor in a way that they were not if they could not see it. Any students lurking in the corridor between lessons were immediately obvious, and teachers felt obliged to go into the corridor and deal with them, at the expense of interrupting their own lessons. Although it might seem preferable, especially to senior managers, that such students are questioned, it should perhaps be acknowledged that this might cause other problems for those provoked to intervene. In some newly built schools, the idea of passive surveillance has been extended to involve staff other than teachers, through locating office space overlooking student circulation areas. The effect of this arrangement on staff who have not be trained or may not feel confident to deal with student misbehaviour needs to be thought through. Having spaces overseen by staff, such as TAs and administrators, who have traditionally maintained a more positive relationship with even quite challenging students may seem ingenious but might serve to threaten those relationships.

Colour

As described in Chapter 3, it is very hard to reach useful conclusions about colour in school premises, since there is little agreement between individuals or between groups of school users in their preferences. Yet the impact that colours make on us as human beings means that there is no shortage of ideas for decoration based on colours which are supposed to be conducive to particular moods or activities. Considering such claims, it is useful to bear in mind an observation made about colour in the workplace: 'Color is one of the least studied aspects of the physical environment, but it nevertheless remains the topic of some of the most optimistic claims about morale and efficiency' (Sundstrom, 1987: 751).

Some newly built schools have recognised that users certainly notice colour-schemes and have made more striking use of colour than has been common in British schools over the last fifty years. Explicit thought is also being given to how colours can be used to give character to particular areas and so aid orientation. For example, a school which has particular social areas for each year group has added to their distinctiveness through the use of strong colours in each area. In another school, there was a desire to signify quadrants of the building, which are linked to curriculum areas, through the use of colour. The decision was made to keep these coloured parts fairly minimal so that the colour scheme as a whole did not become too 'loud', which was achieved through coloured chairs, desk edging and some storage, against a neutral background. It remains to be seen how the contrasting white areas used to some effect in both these schools wear over time (see Figure 7.2). Since research into schools, or other buildings, has been unable to determine which colours are best for particular purposes, it would seem that the most important aspect of these schemes is the sense of ownership they might engender in the school users. Such positive feelings about colour schemes, especially the more striking ones, are surely more likely to develop through a participatory design process, so users feel some involvement in the choices that have been made.

The staffroom

Although staffrooms are generally recognised as important and distinctive spaces within a school, the literature relating to the physical school environment does not often report investigations or analysis of their function. Perhaps because they are not directly involved in teaching and learning interactions, they tend to be overlooked, and this is reflected in the reactions of staff who sometimes claim that the staff room is not an important part of the school since the learners do not go there. With the tendency, mentioned in Chapter 5, of current participatory school design projects to centre on the involvement of students rather than school staff, it seems probable that staffrooms will not be prioritised in school rebuilding. Yet social relationships between staff members

Figure 7.2 Use of colour and contrast in a year group base in a recently built secondary school

are clearly important to the functioning of the school as a whole, particularly when the school is experiencing a period of change. As Andrew Pollard concluded from his primary and middle school case studies, the staffroom is 'the territory of the classroom teacher and a critical area in which confidences are exchanged, tension is released and the staff culture of the school develops' (Pollard, 1985: 20). The nature of these relationships which are developed between staff must be related to the spaces that are provided and the ways that they come to be used.

Traditionally, a single staffroom has been provided. This works well in smaller schools, usually primary schools, where, as described by Pollard, the single room is used for meetings, notice boards, eating and socialising. These room become important hubs, where official communications are centred, through notices and briefings, together with the informal discussions that take place between staff members over breaktime coffee or lunchtime sandwiches. The centrality of these rooms only becomes a problem if some members of staff feel they are excluded from the informal interactions and are, in fact, not included in the formal meetings. This is sometimes the case for support workers, such as TAs and lunchtime supervisors, and can form an important part of their sense of separation and lower status (Sharp, 1994: 125).

A contrasting problem with a single staffroom occurs when staff tend not to use it. This was the case in the secondary school where we conducted an initial consultation as part of the school's redesign (Woolner *et al.*; 2010). The photograph we used of the staffroom showed it empty and staff commented that it usually looked like that. Maps produced by staff further demonstrated that many rarely visited the staff room. When this happens to a school staff room, it will lose its informal role. It will only function as a formal meeting place, with even this usage compromised by the fact that staff are not there very often to read notices or collect post. This often happens in physically larger schools, especially if the premises consists of separate blocks or buildings, and is therefore more commonly seen in secondary schools. A secondary school involved in the Design Council's Schools Renaissance project centred their design project on improving school communications and a key aspect of this was the refurbishment of the staffroom. The intention was to make the space more pleasant, but also more appropriate to staff usage through arranging distinct areas for social interaction and for work, such as marking and preparation (Hall & Wall, 2006).

This failure to use the staffroom in secondary schools should, however, not just be seen in terms of the lack of appeal of an unattractive space too far away. The structuring of secondary school through academic disciplines produces a tendency for teachers to identify with their department and spend their free time with departmental colleagues, often squeezed into preparation rooms or storage areas. These spaces then begin to facilitate the mixture of formal and informal interactions seen in primary school staff rooms. They can also support the mixing of certain teaching and non-teaching staff, principally in subjects such as science and ICT which have dedicated technicians. Yet this strengthening of bonds within subject areas can lead to fragmentation across the school as a whole and resentment from staff outside these apparently insular departments. In particular, non-teaching staff with a more general role, such as SEN TAs or administrators can feel excluded.

Despite these disadvantages, the decision has been made in some recently built secondary schools to embrace and plan for the staff dispersal that often occurs. Accommodation is included in various places across the site for staff to gather, with these rooms referred to as 'subject bases' or intended for staff in particular parts of the building. There is often also an intention for these localised staff meeting places to add to the passive surveillance of students, an aim which, as argued above, is often not fully examined. These staff bases may lead to some mixing of staff from different subject areas, although this is likely to be limited to related disciplines. For example, in one recently completed school, where each wing of the school has a staff base, one of these rooms brings together the food technology and the design and technology staff. Bigger departments, however, such as mathematics and English completely fill a wing so their staff bases are effectively subject bases.

Interestingly, in a school that was completed at the beginning of the twenty-first century, with separate subject bases for staff across the school, a recent addition to the school was a single general staffroom. This seems to have been particularly well received by non-teaching staff, including office staff, lunchtime supervisors and the caretaker, who previously felt that they had nowhere to go for their breaks. In the first year of the new staff room, they made good use of it and commented that doing so made them feel more included in the life and work of the school. What is less clear in this school is how well the new room is functioning as a meeting place for teaching staff.

It would seem then that there is no complete solution to the problem of providing a staff room that fulfils a range of informal and formal functions for the various members of teaching and other staff. Since the use of the staffroom is not obligatory, beyond formal meetings and briefings, it is perhaps more important than in other areas of the school that the potential users feel some ownership of the space or identification with the other people there. This suggests the involvement of staff through the planning and building of this part of the new school. Examination before the rebuild of existing staffroom usage, together with the investigation of why such use, or lack of use, is occurring should help in developing an overview of the aims and intentions of the new staff room provision. This seems very important given the tendency, discussed above, for staff rooms to be overlooked and therefore not planned properly. Then, at later stages of construction, perhaps it would help staff feel that a room was theirs if they could choose fittings or plan the arrangement of furniture.

During the building process

When a school is being completely rebuilt, the central focus during the construction process might seem to be on the physical structure itself, but there is an important social side to this period. This is important to recognise, especially as the construction phase might seem, for those less directly involved, to take a long time. An awareness of the need to develop a feeling of involvement during this time is seen in the efforts made by schools to keep their students, staff and the wider local community informed of progress. This leads to dedicated websites, regular newsletters and displays of photographs and plans, which are updated as building progresses. As argued in Chapter 1, any sense of ownership and community pride in the new school, which these communications may help to engender, should contribute to the school continuing to be appreciated as time passes.

A disadvantage to this encouragement of interest in the new building, however, might be that all eyes seem to be on the new premises taking shape, and a lack of concern is perceived for the existing building and the education which is continuing within. This is particularly unfortunate for the final year students, who will not personally experience the new building. They will be reaching important transitions in their lives, including preparing to move up to the next educational stage or studying for public examinations, and may feel that this key time is being overshadowed.

This sense that everything outside the rebuild is of low priority for the school will be heightened if financial and building management decisions lead to the existing premises becoming increasingly dilapidated. Early evaluation of the BSF programme found that this could indeed be a problem in schools awaiting rebuilding: reductions in money to maintain buildings that are soon to be demolished are compounded by increased littering and vandalism, producing a 'cycle of disengagement from the current schools estate' (PricewaterhouseCoopers, 2008: 66–69). The evaluators suggest that LAs should do more to ensure that schools plan in advance for this difficult financial period, but the problem may extend beyond building maintenance. In a school I visited, one senior teacher complained that training to prepare staff for the new building was dominating professional development and making it very hard to discuss other innovations, such as overhauling the curriculum. Given the hopes of educationalists and LA advisors that school design may act as a catalyst for other change in school, this experience is quite paradoxical.

A final social issue, which is becoming obvious to those most directly involved in the rebuilding process, is the management of relationships between the individuals involved. The development of these relationships between people from very different occupations and professions, with different assumptions and understandings of schools, presents challenges of communication, which have already been touched upon in the discussion of participatory design in Chapters 4 and 5. Once the construction period is started, there will typically be architects and construction professionals interacting on a daily basis with the school's BSF coordinators, who will usually have backgrounds in education, or, in the case of school bursars or business managers, finance. In a school I visited as the new building neared completion, the school staff and the construction company staff emphasised the importance of good working relationships. The school BSF coordinator, an assistant head teacher, and the construction consortium's project manager were clearly on good terms with each another. However, this assistant head teacher who had taken responsibility for BSF also told me about demanding negotiations he had been involved with, which had necessitated a 'steep learning curve' on his part. He emphasised the importance of 'recognising the commercialism of companies you're dealing with' and described negotiations as like 'game-playing'.

The centrality of social interactions and relationships

Although the policy title of building schools for the future might primarily suggest a programme of school construction to engineers and architects, educators may also understand it as implying development of the network of relationships within the school community. A teacher I spoke to about BSF commented that only when the new premises were in place could the real work of building the school itself begin. He evidently understood the school to be more embodied in the relationships between staff and students than in nature of their physical surroundings.

This reaction serves to highlight the more purely social aspects of a school, but, as is clear from the content of this chapter, these relationships also have a physical side. They take place within the setting of the school and will be affected by the design of that setting: meetings between particular individuals or groups of people will be facilitated or hindered by the organization of parts of the school. Conversely, the relationships which are expected or considered normal in a particular school may influence the arrangement of physical space. These influences range from large scale school design decisions based on the needs of social interactions within the existing school to the smaller scale impact of alterations to staffrooms or teaching spaces to make certain interactions more likely. Just as it was argued in the final section above that the construction process itself can be understood in both physical and social terms, the rebuilding of a school implies changes to physical space and to relationships within the school community. It seems vital, during the design process and beyond, that this wider understanding of the school is maintained. Since it seems likely that many of the effects of the school environment on learning will be mediated by interactions between people in the setting, any development of understanding through involvement in physical change should be beneficial to that school community.

8 Rebuilding your school: recognising and adapting what works to fit emerging needs

The relationship of refurbishment to rebuilding

Much of the early publicity given to BSF by both government and the media centred on the complete school rebuilds and entirely new schools which form an important part of the initiative. While this is understandable, it must be remembered that more individual school will experience refurbishment, as opposed to rebuilding, through BSF. Looking beyond BSF, it seems important to develop an understanding of the process of refurbishment. Money spent on refurbishing schools should go further, allowing more schools to benefit and may be a more appropriate response to a stock of schools with more varying needs, and fewer that require complete rebuilding.

It is important, therefore, not to see refurbishment as the poor relation of rebuilding, and, in fact, our current understanding of the learning environment implies that this is not the case. As has been argued repeatedly, it is impossible to identify a school design which will be perfect for the teaching and learning needs of each and every school community. An appropriate setting for a particular school will depend on the needs of the users, which, of course, are not static. Since an effective way to begin to identify these needs is to discuss the existing school, with a view to enhancing successful elements and solving current problems, this process of understanding needs might be easier in a school that is going to be altered not demolished. Although being part of a process of some change, as opposed to radical renewal, might not seem as exciting to school users, it could be more immediately comprehensible. The potential for success of refurbishment is suggested in places by the literature on school environments, where there are clues to its appeal. Eric Pearson, former schools inspector and enthusiast for progressive education, included in his review of 1970s primary school design two case studies of late Victorian schools which were remodelled in the 1970s (Pearson, 1972). From the descriptions and photographs, it is clear that the schools were able to retain many distinctive nineteenth century features which were liked, but, by removing walls, add the open plan elements which were then favoured.

If this vision is accepted, of a school community reflecting on its current priorities and developing plans and intentions to inform improvement of the physical structure of the school, then the chapters of this book dealing with collaborative design are clearly relevant to those involved in either refurbishment or rebuilding. In the previous two chapters, however, there has been something of an emphasis on rebuilds. In those chapters, an attempt was generally made to consider the various elements of the school setting in the context of extensive change to the school as a whole. For example, in discussions of the impact of classroom shape and size, even though classroom level management of space was considered, the altered classroom was assumed to be part of a coherent system of classroom organisation, not just an experimental alteration limited to a particular department. These intentions not with standing, however, it might be anticipated that certain sections of these chapters will be of direct interest to those investigating or involved in school refurbishment. It would be expected that the parts judged relevant will depend on the nature and detail of the refitting which is being examined or planned.

It seems, however, that there are additional aspects to remodelling or refurbishing a school which are not entirely covered by the previous chapters. These projects will perhaps be more self-contained, with distinct limits to their ambitions. If the purpose is to build a new science wing or performing arts block, then it will seem less appropriate to talk about restructuring learning across the school. Where discussions do take such a turn, it will be clear that the suggestions cannot involve physical alterations to other parts of the school, although they might involve changes to organisation, through altering pastoral arrangements or timetabling. It would seem therefore that there is no reason why refurbishing a school should not be a catalyst for change, as it has been argued that rebuilding can be. The detail of the resulting discussions might be different, and there might be more sense of focus or limitation, but it still seems plausible to reflect on the needs and desires of the school community.

This focusing, however, will have implications for the understanding that those involved develop of the process, and perhaps for how the results come to be understood. With this perspective, in the sections which follow, I will discuss aspects of school setting that lend themselves to alteration or improvement, without necessitating a complete rebuild. These examples are drawn from recent school improvement work, mostly taken from schools I have worked with, researched within or visited, but with some links being made to the literature of learning environments where appropriate.

Outside space

One of the areas of the school where stand-alone changes or improvements can most obviously be made is the external space. This is reflected in research and campaigns, which clearly predate BSF, focusing on the improvement of school grounds (e.g. Lucas, 1994; Sheat & Beer, 1994). Yet this interest chimes with contemporary concerns about the relationship of the school to its local community. As two researchers in this area argued more than a decade ago, 'For some members of the community, the school grounds are the only aspect of school life they see … they draw conclusions about the effectiveness of the school and the way in which it is organised and managed' (Sharp & Blatchford, 1994: 193). During the consultation days in a secondary school which I conducted with colleagues, we noted that a photograph we used showing an exterior view of the school tended to elicit overviews and judgments about the school. Being shown the 'view from the neighbourhood' suggested certain issues, often starting from, but going beyond, ideas about general appearance. For example, this photograph prompted some Year 7 students to move from discussing rubbish and the big fences to mention that they felt ashamed of the school, although this was not a common attitude among students or staff (Woolner *et al.*, 2010).

During this consultation, students, teachers and other staff at the school all tended to agree that improvements were needed to the outside space. Ideas centred on a need to make the school grounds more pleasant and design in social spaces, such as 'seats outside so we can have lunch' (a student suggestion). Such reactions could clearly form the beginning of a relatively small scale project to improve the outside space, and, as mentioned above, there is an existing literature within education research suggesting how this might be done. The potential for such initiatives to succeed in their own terms is high, since they can be pursued gradually, with later additions being planned iteratively in response to earlier changes. In turn, this should facilitate involvement and ownership of the school space, perhaps improving social relationships and the culture of the school.

A more focused approach to improving the outdoor environment, and heightening its potential to support learning, may be attempted through the planning of wildlife gardens or vegetable plots. As with the landscaping of school grounds, there are numerous current initiatives in this area, as well as a long established belief in the multiple benefits of school gardening (Dillon *et al.*, 2003). I have been involved in an on-going evaluation of one project to enhance the primary school curriculum which includes a gardening strand (Open Futures, nd). Through this involvement, I have witnessed the impact that gardening can have on the attitude and motivation of many learners, and heard about improved relationships across the school community. Many staff involved in this project also consider that it has had positive effects on learning within the existing curriculum, though it is difficult to establish this conclusively (Woolner & Tiplady, 2009).

Whatever the focus that is adopted by a school in its development of its outside space, it will be of central importance that enhancements are maintained. This might involve repairing and maintaining seating, repainting playground designs and weeding garden areas. If these aspects are allowed to become tatty or look uncared-for, this might well have a negative impact on the school community, perhaps one more immediate and of greater magnitude than the anticipated positive effects of the improvements when new. Also, when implementing changes to the school grounds, it is important that the existing provision is properly examined and understood. Since some of the ways that the outside space is used might not be immediately apparent, particularly to an adult eye, it will be important to involve students of various ages as well as a range of staff in the redevelopment. A case study which shows the potential for omissions researched playground games in the grounds of a nineteenth century primary school. A game which had been played for generations around a distinctive pipe was lost when a mobile classroom was installed against the pipe (Armitage, 2005).

New blocks

In many schools, both now and in the past, capital expenditure has been spent on the construction of new blocks or wings. This may allow a school to update facilities for particular areas of the curriculum or accommodate an increase in student numbers. Although this may allow the precise targetting of resources and encourage improvements to be made in line with definite needs and aspirations, there are also disadvantages to such piecemeal alterations to the premises. The period of construction itself may prove disruptive. The addition of new parts to the school is less likely to produce the problems discussed in the previous chapter, where a cycle of disintegration occurs in the soon to be abandoned old building. Yet the process of building might actually be more disruptive as work is more likely to be taking place within areas still in use. In one school I worked with, the improvements to the arts provision in the school necessitated the school hall being out of use for some months, and the construction work going on in several places across the school was often noisy and dusty.

Once the new areas are in use, there is a potential problem, related to the disengagement observed in school buildings awaiting demolition, of unfavourable comparisons being made between the new and older parts of the school. The wider corridor in the new block, which was studied as an architectural case study and mentioned in previous chapters, resulted in measurably better behaviour and experiences (Ross, 2006). This must surely have served to highlight to the school community, however, the problems occurring in the older, narrower corridors in the school. In a secondary school, the location of particular subject areas in relation to these new and old parts of the schools may encourage more negative student attitudes to certain subjects or even make it more difficult for the school to attract and retain subject specialists. In a primary school, where learners tend to stay in one classroom, decisions about which classes to place in the shiny new rooms will also have the potential to fracture, rather than unite, a school community.

Finally, in planning the addition of new buildings or areas to an existing school, it will be necessary to consider how the premises as a whole will look and be experienced by users (Figure 8.1). Clearly a collection of buildings from different eras can be interesting, and even educational, for students, but the school may end up seeming somewhat disjointed. Management of blocks of very different construction may also prove awkward. They might have varying levels of insulation, complicating the planning of heating or cooling, or contain different fixtures and fittings, which will need different levels of maintenance or replacing at different rates.

Figure 8.1 A school with buildings from different eras linked by a pleasant outdoor seating area

Decoration

As has been argued in previous chapters (in particular in Chapter 3), it is difficult to assess precisely the relationship between cost and benefit within school design, and it seems likely that, in some cases, a relatively cheap alteration may be as effective as a more expensive innovation. Thus it might be found that new decoration within a school could be as well-received as structural alterations, though be considerably less disruptive to implement, and also cheaper. The wider corridor described above seems to have been effective in improving circulation within the school. Yet similar benefits for circulation and student behaviour were claimed for a corridor redecoration carried out by the Design Council, which was intended to make a school corridor seem wider although it did not actually change its width (Hall & Wall, 2006).

Colours, as discussed in earlier chapters, are often claimed to exert particular influences over the perceptions and behaviour of an environment's inhabitants, but there is little reliable evidence for individual colours having certain effects. As described in chapter 6, however, in the context of a rebuilding project, they might be used to give character to the school premises as a whole, or to aid orientation and the distinguishing of areas within the building. Such an approach could also be taken as a central part of a refurbishment of existing school premises. The impact would be expected to be wider if such redecoration is undertaken as part of a bigger initiative, perhaps including changes to the shape of the school day or a rethinking of the curriculum. As ever, the sense that the school community has of ownership and genuine involvement will depend on the participation of a range of school users through the planning and implementing of such change.

The idea of visible changes to the school environment being a part of a more general process of change, innovation or creativity is evident in projects such as those conducted through the Creative Partnerships scheme, for example (Creative Partnerships, 2009). Such approaches to change in school return us to a conception of the school environment as a complex interaction of settings, behaviour and perceptions, where the experienced school is a product as well as a cause of the relationships that exist within its walls.

The wider implications of a refurbishment approach

As these discussions of possible focus for the remodelling of a school suggest, there appear to be some disadvantages to such an approach to change in the learning environment. Any project where some improvements are made but other aspects left unchanged will tend to highlight the unchanged parts. This could produce negative responses, particularly where there is a clear physical distinction between improved spaces and unchanged areas. In this way, making some improvements might lead to the school community being less generally satisfied with the educational environment. There are some suggestions in the research into learning spaces of such a reaction to limited improvement. For instance, a study in American elementary schools found that when the classroom was arranged to provide more places of privacy for learners, the children seemed to be less satisfied with the provision of private spaces (Ahrentzen & Evans, 1984).

It is this tendency, however, for users to become more critical which fuels the potential, often remarked upon, for the making of some limited change to act as a catalyst for other change. Within the context of the school as a complex organisation, as well as a physical setting, even a complete rebuild will leave some aspects of the learning environment unchanged. It would seem that the important factor in both rebuilding and refurbishing projects is the use that is made of the raised levels of awareness and critical understanding of the everyday functioning of the school which is usually taken for granted. Where outlets are not provided for these reactions to the enacted changes and resulting ideas for further changes, it seems likely that people will start to feel unappreciated and not in control, with negative consequences for the school community.

If, in contrast, there is commitment to the possibility of ongoing change and experimentation within the school, the questions raised by one change or innovation are likely to have a more positive effect. It is an association with gradual or iterative change which makes refurbishment seem more manageable in this respect than a complete school rebuild. Yet, any opportunities to make targetted improvements to a school environment, either through remodelling aspects of an existing school or through adjustments to a newer building, could produce useful and appreciated changes. An example of adjustment within a relatively new school was mentioned in the previous chapter, where a general staffroom was added to the premises some years after construction, to the satisfaction of many staff members.

To conclude, then, it would seem that any changes of whatever scale made to the learning environment provided by the school premises have, by necessity, wider implications. As has been argued throughout this book, these effects should be understood in terms of the physical design of space and the organisation of people, as well as in terms of relationships between those people and their facilitation of learning. Successful change will attempt to understand impacts on the physical surroundings and on the experience of the users, together with appreciating the complexities of the dynamic relationships between these aspects. Such successful involvement in change is perhaps best understood as an iterative process, but might be present in the stages of a rebuilding project, or underpin a useful refurbishment. In both cases, the sense of possibility and potential is founded on the complexity of the relationship between school and users. Both research evidence and everyday experience suggests that this relationship will never be completely defined for a particular school and so the process of developing the individual learning environment can never be finished.

References

Adams, E. and Ward, C. (1982) *Art and the built environment: a teacher's approach*, Harlow, Published for the Schools Council by Longman

Ahman, M., Lundin, A., Musabas¡c, V. & Soderman, E. (2000) 'Improved health after intervention in a school with moisture problems', *Indoor Air*, 10, 57–62.

Ahrentzen, S. and Evans, G.W. (1984) 'Distraction, Privacy and Classroom Design'. *Environment and Behaviour* **16**(4): 437–454

Alexander, R. (1992) *Policy and practice in primary education*, London: Routledge

Armitage, M. (2005) 'The Influence of School Architecture and Design on the Outdoor Play Experience within the Primary School', *Paedagogica Historica*, 41: 535–553

Arnstein, S.R. (1969) 'A Ladder of Citizen Participation'. *Journal of the American Institute of planners* **5**(4): 216–224

Arzi, H.J. (1998) 'Enhancing science education through laboratory environments: more than walls, benches and widgets'. In B.J. Fraser and G.Tobin (eds) *International handbok of science education*, 595–608. Dordrecht, Netherlands: Kluwer

Asprino, A., Broadbent, G.H. et al. (1981) 'A critical examination of design failures in buildings and their relation to design processes'. *Design: Science: Method*, R. Jacques and J.A. Powell. Guildford: Westbury House

Barnitt, H. (2003) 'Lighting for the future', *Building Services Journal: the Magazine for the CIBSE*, 25(1), 38–39

Bennett, N., Andreae, J. et al. (1980) *Open plan schools*, Windsor: Schools Council

Berry, M.A. (2002) 'Healthy school environment and enhanced educational performance: The case of Charles Young elementary school', Washington, DC: Carpet and Rug Institute

Boman, E. and Enmarker, I. (2004) 'Factors affecting pupils' noise annoyance in schools: the building and testing of models', *Environment and Behavior*, 36(2), 207–228

Blatchford, P., Bassett, P., Brown, P., Martin, C., Russell, A. and Webster, R. (2007) 'Deployment and impact of support staff in schools report' (Strand 1, Wave 2). London: DCSF

Blatchford, P. and Sharp, S. (1994) (eds) *Breaktime and the School*, London: Routledge

Blundell Jones, P., Petrescu, D. and Till, J. (2005) *Architecture and Participation*, Abingdon Oxon / New York: Spon

Bragg, S. and Buckingham, D. (2008) '"Scrapbooks" as a resource in media research with young people'. In P. Thomson (ed.) *Doing Visual Research with Children and Young People*, London: Routledge.

Brennan, A., Chugh, J. S. and Kline, T. (2002) 'Traditional versus open office design: a longitudinal field study', *Environment and Behavior*, 34(3), 279–299

Brighton and Hove city Council (2003) Participation http://www.brighton-hove.gov.uk/index.cfm?request=c1131710 (accessed 11.5.09)

Bross, C. and Jackson, K. (1981) 'Effects of room colour on mirror tracing by junior high school girls', *Perceptual and Motor Skills*, **52**:767–770.

Buckley, J., Schneider, M. and Shang, Y. (2004) *LAUSD school facilities and academic performance*, Los Angeles: Unified School District

Bullock, N. (2002) *Building the Post-War World*, London: Routledge

Bunn, R. (2008) 'A Victorian school, a 1970s school and a post-millennium sustainable school. Which one has the lowest carbon footprint?' Bracknell: BSRIA

Burke, C. and Grosvenor, I. (2003) *The School I'd Like*, London: RoutledgeFalmer

Burke, C. (2007) 'The View of the Child: Releasing "visual voices" in the design of learning environments'. *Discourse: studies in the cultural politics of education*, **28**(3): 359–372

Burleigh (2009) School website http://www.burleigh.herts.sch.uk Accessed 20.10.09
CABE (2006) 'Assessing secondary school design quality'. London, CABE
Canter, D. and Donald, I. (1987) 'Environmental psychology in the UK', in: D. Stockol & I. Altman (eds) *Handbook of envoronmental psychology*, Vol 2, New York: Wiley
Clark, A (2005) 'Talking and listening to children'. In M. Dudek (ed.) *Children's Spaces*, Oxford: Elsevier/ Architectural Press
Clark, C and Uzzell, D.L. (2006) 'The socio-environmental affordances of adolescents' environments'. in C. Spencer and M. Blades (eds) *Children and their Environments*, Cambridge: Cambridge University Press
Clark, H. (2002) 'Building Education: The role of the physical environment in enhancing teaching and research'. London, Institute of Education
Clark, J. (2004) 'Participatory research with children and young people: philosophy, possibilities and perils', *Action Research Expeditions*, 4(Nov), 1–18
Clift, S., Hutchings, R. and Povey, R. (1984) Short Reports *Educational Research*, 26 (3), 208–212
Cohen, S., Evans, G.W., Krantz, D.S. and Stokols, D. (1980) 'Physiological, motivational and cognitive effects of aircraft noise on children moving from the laboratory to the field', *American Psychologist*, 35(3), 231–243
Cohen, S. and Trostle, S.L. (1990) 'Young Children's Preferences for School Related Physical-Environmental Setting Characteristcs'. *Environment and Behavior* **22**(6): 753–766
Comely, G., Goddard, T. and Hill, S. (2005) (eds) *A–Z sketchbook of school build and design*, London: SchoolWorks
Cooper, I. (1981) 'The Politics of Education and Architectural Design: the instructive example of British primary education'. *British Educational Research Journal* 7(2): 125–136
Cooper, I. (1985) 'Teachers' assessments of primary school buildings: the role of the physical environment in education'. *British Educational Research Journal*, **11**(3): 253–269
Creative Partnerships (2009) http://www.creative-partnerships.com Accessed 20.10.09
Cuban, L. (2001) *Oversold and Underused: Computers in the Classroom*, Cambridge, MA: Harvard University Press
Curtis, E. (2003) *School Builders*, Chichester: Wiley
David, T. G. (1975) 'Environmental literacy'. In T.G. David and B.D. Wright (eds) *Learning environments*, Chicago, University of Chicago Press
Design Council (2005) Learning Environments Campaign Prospectus From the Inside Looking Out. London: Design Council http://www.designcouncil.org.uk/en Accessed 18.7.09
DfES (1962) The School Building Survey 1962, London: HMSO.
DfES (2002) Schools for the Future: Designs for Learning Communities Building Bulletin 95. London
DfES (2004) Schools for the Future: Exemplar Designs: concepts and ideas. London: DfES
DfES (2004b) Every Child Matters Change for Children London: TSO
DfES (2006) Design of Sustainable Schools Case Studies. London: TSO
Dillon, J., Richardson, M., Sanders, D., Teamey, K. and Benefield, P. (2003) 'Improving the understanding of food, farming and land management amongst school-age children: a literature review'. London: NFER.
Donovan, J.J. (1921) *School architecture: principles and practice*. New York: MacMillan
Douglas, D. and R. Gifford (2001) 'Evaluation of the physical classroom by students and professors: a lens model approach'. *Educational Research* **43**(3): 295–30
Dudek, M. (2000) *Architecture of Schools*, Oxford: Architectural Press
Dudek, M. (2005) (ed) *Children's Spaces*, Oxford: Elsevier/Architectural Press
Durán-Narucki, V. (2008) 'School building condition, school attendance, and academic achievement in New York City public schools: A mediation model'. *Journal of Environmental Psychology*, **28**: 278–286
Earthman, G. I. (2004) Prioritization of 31 criteria for school building adequacy. Available online at: http://www.schoolfunding.info/policy/facilities/ACLUfacilities_report1-04.pdf Accessed 20.10.09
Engelbrecht, K. (2003) 'The Impact of Colour on Learning'. Available online at: http://web.archive.org/web/20040218065036/http://www.merchandisemart.com/neocon/NeoConConfPro/W305.pdf Accessed 20.10.09

England, Central Advisory Council for Education (1967) 'Children and their primary schools'. A report of the Central Advisory Council for Education, England. London
Estyn (2007) 'An evaluation of performance of schools before and after moving into new buildings or significantly refurbished premises'. Cardiff, Estyn
Evans, G.W. and Maxwell, L. (1997) 'Chronic noise exposure and reading deficits. The mediating effects of language acquisition', *Environment and Behaviour*, 29(5), 638–656
Fell, G. (1994) 'You're only a dinner lady! A case study of the SALVE lunchtime organiser project'. In P. Blatchford and S. Sharp (eds) *Breaktime and the School*, London: Routledge
Fielding, M. (2001a) 'Beyond the Rhetoric of Student Voice: new departures or new constraints in the transformation of 21st century schooling'. *FORUM*, 43, 2, 100–109
Fielding, M. (2001b) 'Students as radical agents of change' *Journal of Educational Change*, 2, 123–141
Finmere (nd) The New School http://www.shelswellparishes.info/finmere/finmerehistory/ Accessed 20.10.09
Fisher, K. (2001) 'Building better outcomes: the impact of school infrastructure on student outcomes and behaviour'. Canberra, Australia: Department of Education, Training and Youth Affairs
Fisher, R. and Larkin, S. (2008) 'Pedagogy or Ideological struggle? An examination of pupils' and Teachers' Expectations for Talk in the Classroom'. *Language and Education*, 22 (1) 1–16
Flutter, J. (2006) '"This place could help you learn": student participation in creating better learning environments'. *Educational Review* **58**(2): 183–193
Flutter, J. and Rudduck, J. (2004) *Consulting Pupils: What's in it for Schools?* London, RoutledgeFalmer
Fraser, B.J. (1984) 'Differences Between Preferred and Actual Classroom Environment as Perceived by Primary Students and Teachers'. *British Journal of Educational Psychology* 54: 336–339
Frost, R. and Holden, G. (2008) 'Student voice and future schools: building partnerships for student participation' *Improving Schools* 11 (1) 83–95
Fullan, M. (2001) *The new meaning of educational change* (3rd ed) New York: Teachers College Press
Galton, M., Hargreaves, L., Comber, C., Wall, D. and Pell, A. (1999) *Inside the primary classroom: 20 years on*, London: Routledge
Goulding (2007) 'Digital Media Artists working with teachers'. Paper presented at BERA 2008, 3–6 September, Edinburgh
Greany, T. (2005) Foreword. In S. Higgins, E. Hall, K. Wall, P. Woolner and C. McCaughey (2005). *The Impact of School Environments: A literature review*. London: Design Council
Gump, P.V. (1975) 'Operating environments in schools of open and traditional design'. In T. G. David and B. D. Wright (eds) *Learning environments*. Chicago: UCP University of Chicago Press.
Gump, P.V. (1987) 'School and classroom environments', in: D. Stockol and I. Altman (eds) *Handbook of environmental psychology*, Vol. 1 (New York, Wiley)
Haines, M.M., Stansfeld, S.A., Brentnall, J., Berry, B., Jiggins, M. and Hygge, S. (2001a) 'The West London Schools Study: the effects of chronic aircraft noise exposure on child health', *Psychological Medicine*, 31, 1385–1396
Haines, M.M., Stansfeld, S.A., Job, R.F.S., Berglund, B. and Head, J. (2001b) 'Chronic aircraft noise exposure, stress responses, mental health and cognitive performance in school children', *Psychological Medicine*, 31, 265–277
Hall, E. and. Wall, K. (2006) *Schools Renaissance Evaluation*, Newcastle University
Hall, I and Higgins, S. (2005) 'Primary school students' perceptions of interactive whiteboards'. *Journal of Computer Assisted Learning*, 21, 102–117
Hallam, S. (1996) *Improving school attendance* Oxford: Heinemann Educational.
Hart, R.A. (1987) Children's participation in planning and design. *Spaces for Children: The built environment and child development*, C.S. Weinstein and T.G. David. New York, Plenum Press
Hart, R. (1997) Children's Participation: the theory and practice of involving young citizens in community development and environmental care. London: Earthscan
Hartnell-Young, E. and Fisher, T. (2007) 'Circling the Square; six activities for listening to teachers and students'. Nottingham: Learning Sciences Research Institute and School of Education, University of Nottingham

Hastings, N. (1995) Seats of learning, *Support for Learning*, 10(1), 8–11
Hathaway, W.E. (1994) *A study into the effects of types of light on children – a case of daylight robbery*
Heschong Mahone Group (2003) 'Windows and Classrooms: A Study of Student Performance and the Indoor Environment', Califonia Energy Commission
Higgins, S., Hall, E., Wall, K., Woolner, P. and McCaughey, C. (2005) *The Impact of School Environments: A literature review*. London, Design Council
Horne, S.C. (1999) 'Classroom environment and its effects on the practice of teachers'. PhD thesis, University of London
Horne-Martin, S. (2002) 'The classroom environment and its effects on the practice of teachers'. *Journal of Environmental Psychology* **22**(1–2): 139–156
Horne Martin, S. (2006) 'The classroom environment and children's performance – is there a relationship?' in C. Spencer and M. Blades (eds) *Children and their Environments*, Cambridge: Cambridge University Press
Hygge, S. (2003) 'Classroom experiments on the effects of different noise sources and sound levels on long-term recall and recognition in children', *Applied Cognitive Psychology*, 17, 895–914
IDEA (1970) *The open plan school*, Dayton, Ohio: Institute for Development of Educational Activities
Jamieson, P., Taylor, P.G. et al., (2000) 'Place and Space in the Design of New Learning Environments'. *Higher Education Research & Development* **19**(2): 221–236
Jones, K. (2003) *Education in Britain: 1944 to the present*, Oxford: Polity
Karpen, D. (1993) 'Full spectrum polarized lighting: an option for light therapy boxes'. Paper presented at 101st Annual Convention of the American Psychological Association, Toronto
Kingsbury, C. (2006) http://www.chkingsbury.plus.com/hills Accessed 10.8.06.
Khattar, M., Shirey, D. and Raustad, R. (2003) 'Cool & dry – Dual-path approach for a Florida school', *Ashrae Journal*, 45(5), 58–60
Killeen, J.P., Evans, G.W. and Danko, S. (2003) 'The role of permanent student artwork in students' sense of ownership in an elementary school', *Environment and Behavior*, 35(2), 250–263.
Kimmel, R., Dartsch, P., Hildenbrand, S., Wodarz, R. and Schmahl, F. (2000) 'Pupils' and teachers' health disorders after renovation of classrooms in a primary school', *Gesundheitswesen*, 62(12), 660–664
Kirby, P. (2002) 'Measuring the magic? Evaluating and researching young people's participation in public decision making'. London: Carnegie Young People Initiative
Kjellberg, A., Landstrom, U., Tesarz, M., Soderberg, L. and Akerlund, E. (1996) 'The effects of non-physical noise characteristics, ongoing task and noise sensitivity on annoyance and distraction due to noise at work', *Journal of Environmental Psychology*, 16(2), 123–136
Knez, I. (1995) 'Effects of indoor lighting on mood and cognition', *Journal of Environmental Psychology*, 15(1), 39–51
Knez, I. (2001) 'Effects of colour of light on nonvisual psychological processes', *Journal of Environmental Psychology*, 21(3), 201–208
Knez, I. and Hygge, S. (2002) 'Irrelevant speech and indoor lighting: effects on cognitive performance and self-reported affect', *Applied Cognitive Psychology*, 16, 709–718
Könings, K.D., Van Zundert, M.J., Brand-Gruwel, S. and Van Merriënboer, J.J.G. (2007) 'Participatory design in secondary eductaion: is it a good idea? Students' and teachers' opinions on its desirability and feasibility'. *Educational Studies* **33**(4): 445–465
Kumar, R., O'Malley, P.M. and Johnston, L.D. (2008) 'Association between Physical Environment of Secondary Schools and Student Problem Behaviour'. *Environment and Behavior*, **40**(4): 455–486
Kytta, M. (2006) 'Environmental child-friendliness in the light of the Bullerby Model' in C. Spencer and M. Blades (eds) *Children and their Environments*, Cambridge: Cambridge University Press
Lawn, M. (1999) Designing Teaching: the classroom as technology. *Silences and Images: the social history of the classroom*, I. Grosvenor, M. Lawn and K. Rousmaniere. New York: Peter Lang.
Leaman, A. and Bordass, B. (2001) 'Assessing building performance in use 4: the Probe occupant surveys and their implications'. *Building Research and Information*, 29 (2) 129–143

Lercher, P., Evans, G.W. and Meis, M. (2003) 'Ambient noise and cognitive processes among primary schoolchildren', *Environment and Behavior*, 35(6), 725–735

Lodge, C. (2005) 'From hearing voices to engaging in dialogue: problematising student participation in school improvement'. *Journal of Educational Change*, 6, 125–146

Lodge, C. (2007) 'Regarding learning: Children's drawings of learning in the classroom ' *Learning Environments Research 10*: 145–156.

Loughlin, C.E. and Suina, J.H. (1982) *The learning environment: an instructional strategy* (New York, Teachers College Press)

Lucas, B. (1994) 'The power of school grounds: the philiosophy and practice of learning through landscapes'. In P. Blatchford and S. Sharp (eds) *Breaktime and the School*. London: Routledge

Lundquist, P., Holmberg, K., Burström, L. and Landström, U. (2003) 'Sounds levels in classrooms and effects on self-reported mood among school children', *Perceptual and Motor Skills*, 96, 1289–1299

Lundquist, P., Kjellberg, A. and Holmberg, K. (2002) 'Evaluating effects of the classroom environment: development of an instrument for the measurement of self-reported mood among school children', *Journal of Environmental Psychology*, 22, 289–293

Maclure, S. (1985) *Educational development and school building: aspects of public policy 1945–73*, Harlow, Longman

Markus, T.A. (1996) 'Early nineteenth century school space and ideology'. *Paedagogica Historia*, **30**(11): 9–50

Martin, B. (1952) *School Buildings 1945–1951*, London, Crosby Lockwood

Marx, A., Fuhrer, U. and Hartig, T. (2000) 'Effects of classroom seating arrangements on children's question-asking', *Learning Environments Research*, 2, 249–263

Maslow, A. H. & Mintz, N. L. (1956) 'Effects of esthetic surroundings: initial effects of three esthetic conditions upon perceiving "energy" and "well-being" in faces', *Journal of Psychology*, 41, 247–254.

Matthews, H. and Limb, M. (2003) 'Another White Elephant? Youth Councils as Democratic Structures Space and Polity' 7, 2, 173–192

Maxwell, L.E. (2000) 'A Safe and Welcoming School : What Students, Teachers, and Parents Think'. *Journal of Architectural and Planning Research*, **17**(4): 271–282

Maxwell, L.E. and G.W. Evans (2000) 'The effects of noise on pre-school children's pre-reading skills'. *Journal of Environmental Psychology*, **20**: 91–97

McCarter, S. (2009) 'How Conceptualisations of Learning are Revealed by the use of Carpet Space in Primary Schools' Unpublished D.Ap.E.P. Thesis Newcastle University

McGonigal, J.A. (1999) 'Constructing a learning environment that scaffolds science inquiry in first grade'. *Learning Environments Research*, **2**: 21–41

McMillan, M.A. (1983) *An Open Question*, Edinburgh, Scottish Council for Research in Education.

McNamara, D. and Waugh, D. (1993) 'Classroom organisation', *School Organization*, 13(1), 41–50

McSporran, E., Butterworth, Y. and Rowson, V.J. (1997) 'Sound field amplification and listening behaviour in the classroom', *British Educational Research Journal*, 23(1), 81–92

Mills, E.D., (ed.) (1976) Planning: Buildings for Education, Culture and Science. London, Newnes-Butterworths

Mitchell, J. (2008) 'Building Schools for the Future: setting the hares running'. *FORUM*, **50**(2): 243–

Moore, G.T. (1979) 'Environment-behavior studies'. In J.C. Snyder and A.J. Cantanese (eds) Introduction to architecture New York, McGraw-Hill

Moore, R. and Muller, J. (1999) The Discourse of 'Voice' and the Problem of Knowledge in the Sociology of Education, *British Journal of Education*, 20 (2) 189–206

Muijs and Reynolds, (2001) *Effective teaching: evidence and practice* London: Chapman

NUT (England) (1974) Open Planning: A report with special reference to primary schools. London: NUT

Ofsted (2001) *Annual report 1999/2000.* Available at: *http://www.archive.official-documents.co.uk/document/ofsted/hc102/102.htm* Accessed 19.11.09

Open Futures (nd) www.openfutures.info/index.htm

Ornstein, S.W. (1997) 'Postoccupancy evaluation performed in elementary and high schools of Greater Sao Paulo, Brazil. THe occupants and the quality of the school environment'. *Environment and Behavior*, **29**(2): 236–263
Ouston, J., Maughan, B. and Rutter, M. (1991) 'Can Schools Change? II: Practice in Six London Secondary Schools'. *School Effectiveness and School Improvement*, 2,1, 3–13
Panagiotopoulou, G., Christoulas, K., Papanckolaou, A. and Mandroukas, K. (2004) 'Classroom furniture dimensions and anthropometric measures in primary school', *Applied Ergonomics*, 35(2), 121–128
Parcells, C., Stommel, M. and Hubbard, R.P. (1999) 'Mismatch of classroom furniture and student body dimensions. Empirical findings and health implications', *Journal of Adolescent Health*, 24(4), 265–273
Parnell, R., Cave, V. and Torrington, J (2008) 'School design: opportunities through collaboration' *CoDesign*, 4, 4, 211–224
Pearson, E. (1972) Trends in School Design. *British Primary Schools Today*, A.-A. P. E. Project.London, Macmillan. 2
Pearson, E. (1975) *School Building and Educational Change*, Paris, OECD
Pollard, A (1985) *The social world of the primary school*, London: Holt
Pollard, A. (2008) 'Knowledge transformation and impact: aspirations and experiences from TLRP' *Cambridge Journal of Education* 38, 1, 5–22
Poulton, E.C. (1978) 'A new look at the effects of noise: a rejoinder', *Psychological Bulletin*, 85(5), 1068–1079
PricewaterhouseCoopers (2000) Building Performance: An empirical assessment of the relationship between schools capital investment and pupil performance, DfEE
PricewaterhouseCoopers (2007) Evaluation of BSF-1st Annual Report DCSF
PricewaterhouseCoopers (2008) Evaluation of BSF-2nd Annual Report DCSF
Proshansky, E. and Wolfe, M. (1975) The physical setting and open education, in: T.G. David & B.D. Wright (eds) *Learning environments* Chicago: University of Chicago Press
Read, M., Sugawara, A.I. and Brandt, J.A. (1999) 'Impact of space and color in the physical environment on preschool children's cooperative behavior', *Environment and Behavior*, 31(3), 413–428
Richardson, T. and Connelly, S. (2005) 'Reinventing public participation: planning in the age of consensus'. In P. Blundell Jones, D. Petrescu and J. Till (eds) Abingdon *Architecture and Participation* Oxon / New York: Spon
Riddle, M.D. and Arnold, M.V. (2007) The Day Experience Method: A Resource Kit http://www.matthewriddle.com/papers/Day_Experience_Resource_Kit.pdf Accessed 27.8.09
Rivlin, L.G. and M. Rothenberg (1976) 'The Use of Space in Open Classrooms'. In H.M. Proshansky, W H. Ittelson and L.G. Rivlin (eds) *Environmental Psychology: People and Their Physical Settings*, New York, Holt, Rinehart & Winston.
Rivlin, L.G. and Weinstein, C.S. (1984) 'Educational issues, school settings, and environmental psychology', *Journal of Environmental Psychology*, 4, 347–364
Rivlin, L.G. and Wolfe, M. (1985) *Institutional settings in children's lives* New York: Wiley
Rosen, K.G. and Richardson, G. (1999) 'Would removing indoor air particulates in children's environments reduce rate of absenteeism – hypothesis', *The Science of the Total Environment*, 234, 87–93
Robson, E. (2001) The Routes Project: disadvantaged young people interviewing their peers In National Youth Agency (eds) *Young People as Researchers: possibilities, problems and politics*
Robson, P.A. (1911) *School-Planning*, London, Nicholson-Smith
Rockett, M. and Percival, S. (2002) *Thinking for Learning*, Stafford, Network Educational Press
Ross, S. (2006) 'How does the design of circulation spaces in secondary schools affect student behaviour?' Unpublished MA thesis Inchbald School of Design/University of Wales
Rudd, P., Reed, F. and Smith, P. (2008) 'The Effects of the School Environment on Young People's Attitudes to Education and Learning'. Slough: NFER.
Rudduck, J. (1980) 'Insights into the Process of Dissemination' *British Educational Research Journal*, 6, 2, 139–146

Rutter, M., Maughan, B., Mortimore, P. and Ouston, J. (1979) *Fifteen thousand hours: secondary schools and their effects on children* (London, Open Books)
Saint, A. (1987) *Towards a Social Architecture*, Avon, Bath Press
Salame, P. and Wittersheim, G. (1978) 'Selective noise disturbance of the information input in shortterm memory', *Quarterly Journal of Experimental Psychology*, 30, 693–704
Schapiro, B. (2001) National survey of public school teachers, The Carpet and Rug Institute and The International Interior Design Association Foundation
Seaborne, M. (1971) *The English school: its architecture and organization Vol. 1: 1370–1870*, London, Routledge & Kegan Paul.
Seaborne, M. and Lowe, R. (1977) *The English school: its architecture and organization: Vol. 2: 1870–1970*. London, Routledge and Kegan Paul.
Seymour, J. (2001) *SchoolWorks tool kit* London: SchoolWorks
Sharp, S. (1994) 'Training schemes for lunchtime supervisors in the UK'. In P. Blatchford and S. Sharp (eds) *Breaktime and the School*, London: Routledge
Sharp, S. and Blatchford, P. (1994) 'Understanding and changing school breaktime behaviour'. In P. Blatchford and S. Sharp (eds) *Breaktime and the School*, London: Routledge
Sheat, L.G. and Beer, A.R. (1994) 'Giving pupils an effective voice in the design and use of their school grounds'. In P. Blatchford and S. Sharp (eds) *Breaktime and the School*, London: Routledge
Shield, B. and Dockrell, J. (2004) 'External and internal noise surveys of London primary schools', *Journal of the Acoustical Society of America*, 115(2), 730–738
Smedje, G. and Norback, D. (2001) 'Irritants and allergens at school in relation to furnishings and cleaning'. *Indoor Air*, 11, 127–133
Smith, H.J., Higgins, S., Wall, K. and Miler, J. (2005) 'Interactive whiteboards: boon or bandwagon? A critical review of the literature'. *Journal of Computer Assisted Learning*, 21, 91–101
Sommer, R. and Olsen, H. (1980) The soft classroom, *Environment and Behavior*, 12(1), 3–16
Sorrell, J. (2005) *Joinedupdesignforschools*, London: Merrell
Spring, M. (2004). 'Sexy Education'. *Building*, (20.2.04): 24–28
Stansfeld, S.A. and Matheson, M. (2003) 'Noise pollution: non-auditory effects on health', *British Medical Bulletin*, 68, 243–257
Sundstrom, E. (1987) 'Work environments: offices and factories', in: D. Stockol and I. Altman (eds) *Handbook of Environmental Psychology*, New York, Wiley
Tanner, C.K. (2000) 'The influence of school architecture on academic achievement'. *Journal of Educational Administration* **38,**(4): 309–330
Tanner, C.K. and Langford, A. (2002) 'The importance of interior design elements as they relate to student outcomes'. Available online at: http://www.coe.uga.edu/sdpl/research/SDPLStudiesInProgress/criann02elem.html Accessed 20.10.09
Thomson, P. (2008) *Doing Visual Research with Children and Young People*, London: Routledge
Thomson, P. (2007) *Whole school change: a review of the literature*, London: Arts Council England
Till, J. (2005) 'The negotiation of hope', In P. Blundell Jones, D. Petrescu and J. Till (eds) Abingdon *Architecture and Participation*, Oxon / New York, Spon
Todd, L (2007) *Partnerships for inclusive education: a critical approach to collaborative working*, London; New York, NY: RoutledgeFalmer
United Nations Convention on the Rights of the Child (1989) *UN General Assembly Resolution 44/25. Online: www.unhchr.ch/html/menu3/b/k2crc [accessed 12 June 2005]*
Varga-Atkins, T. and O'Brien, M. (2009) 'From drawings to diagrams: maintaining researcher control during graphic elicitation in qualitative interviews', *International Journal of Research and Method in Education*, 32(1): 53–67
Veitch, J.A. (1997) 'Revisiting The performance and mood effects of information about lighting and fluorescent lamp type', *Journal of Environmental Psychology*, 17(3), 253–262
Veitch, J.A. and McColl, S.L. (2001) 'A critical examination of perceptual and cognitive effects attributed to full-spectrum fluorescent lighting', *Ergonomics* 44(3), 255–279

Vincent, C. (1993) 'Community Participation? The establishment of 'City's' Parents' Centres'. *British Educational Research Journal*, 19, 3, 227–241
Walker, J. and Clark, J. (2000) *Changeways: Artists in Probation*, Newcastle: Centre for Family Studies
Wall, K. (2008) 'Understanding Metacognition through the use of Pupil Views Templates: Pupil Views of Learning to Learn', *Thinking Skills and Creativity*, 3: 23–33
Ward, L. (2004) 'A school's great expectations', *The Guardian*, 14 September
Weinstein, C.S. (1979) 'The Physical Environment of the School : A Review of the Research'. *Review of Educational Research*, **49**(4): 577–610
Weinstein, C.S. and David, T.G. (eds) (1987) *Spaces for children: the built environment and child development*, New York: Plenum
Wheldall and Lam, Y.Y. (1987) 'Rows versus tables II. The effects of two classroom seating arrangementson classroom disruption rate, on-task behaviour and teacher behaviour in three special school classes', *Educational Psychology*, 7(4), 303–312
Wheldall, K., Morris, M., Vaughan, P. and Ng, Y.Y. (1981) 'Rows versus tables: an example of the use of behavioural ecology in two classes of eleven-year-old children', *Educational Psychology*, 1(2), 171–184
Woolner, P., Clark, J. and Thomas, U. (2008) 'Using visual activities to mediate a learning conversation about how a school community regards its premises'. Paper presented at BERA 2008, 3–6 September, Edinburgh
Woolner, P. and Hall, E. (2006) 'Evaluating the role of the artist in Building Schools for the Future'. Newcastle upon Tyne: Arts Council England North East / Newcastle University
Woolner, P., Hall, E., Wall, K., Higgins, S., Blake, A. and McCaughey, C. (2005) 'School building programmes: motivations, consequences and implications'. Reading: CfBT
Woolner, P., Hall, E., Clark, J., Tiplady, L., Thomas, U. and Wall, K. (2010). 'Pictures are necessary but not sufficient: using a range of visual methods to engage users about school design', *Learning Environments Research*, 13(1) 1–22
Woolner, P., Hall, E., Higgins, S., McCaughey, C. and Wall, K. (2007a) 'A sound foundation? What we know about the impact of environments on learning and the implications for Building Schools for the Future'. *Oxford Review of Education*, **33**(1): 47–70
Woolner, P., Hall, E., Wall, K. and Dennison, D. (2007b) 'Getting together to improve the school environment: user consultation, participatory design and student voice'. *Improving Schools*, **10**: 233–248
Woolner, P. and Tiplady, L. (2009) 'School gardening as a potential activity for improving science learning in primary schools'. Paper presented at BERA 2009, 2–5 September, Manchester
Wright, S. (2004) 'User Involvement in School Building Design'. *FORUM*, 46, 1, 41–44
Young, E., Green, H.A., Roehrich-Patrick, L., Joseph, L. and Gibson, T. (2003) *Do K–12 school facilities affect education outcomes?* (The Tennessee Advisory Commission on Intergovernmental Relations)
Zandvliet, D. and Straker, L. (2001) 'Physical and psychosocial aspects of the learning environment in information technology rich classrooms', *Ergonomics*, 44(9), 838–857

Index